Look Up
and
Beyond

ALSO BY JESSICA JANNIERE

My Colored World: A Memoir

Look Up and Beyond

Effective Strategies To Become Resilient, Overcome Adversity
and Create A Powerful Future

By Jessica Janniere

The author gratefully acknowledges permission to reprint the following:

"Don't Quit" by John Greenleaf Whittier

ISBN-13: 978-0-692-04163-5

Please visit www.jessicajanniere.com for more information regarding our programs.

Facebook: @jessicajanniere1

Instagram: @jessicajanniere

Email Address: jessicajanniere1@gmail.com

Praise for *Look Up and Beyond* (Student Edition)

"*Look Up and Beyond* offers the real-life struggles Jessica endured throughout her youth. Today, many young people struggle with these same issues often alone and in silence. The power of this book is the message of how she overcomes these struggles. Through the power of journal writing, students reading this book will be able to apply these life-changing strategies to their daily lives. This will allow their physical and emotional adversities to be transformed into healing to look up and beyond their current situations to fulfill their life-long purpose." ~ *Latishia M. Towles, Educator, and New York City School Principal*

"As a school counselor, I witness first-hand the various challenges and adversity our youth are faced with on a daily basis. Jessica's book is definitely one of those gems that will capture the attention of students, and many will be able to relate to Jessica's story in one way or another. If you want to teach and show your students what it means to overcome obstacles, rise to the top, and live the life of their dreams, even when their current situation is telling them otherwise, this book is the *perfect* tool to set that foundation." ~ *Rockell Bartoli, High School Counselor*

"I recommend this book to anyone, but especially young people going through life challenges and needing something to look up to with hope, reality, self-preservation, and purpose. I'm happy Jessica talked about the realities of her experiences that led her to think of and attempt suicide to end her life from pain because many students are living these experiences and need something real to connect with to help them through it; this book is a good resource for that. Be comforted, inspired, and motivated by the words from experience." ~ *Brett Scudder, President/Chairman, The Suicide Institute and NYC Suicide Council*

"The book, *Look Up and Beyond*, is an intriguing read that will assist young people in coping with the issues that many of them face and ways in which to handle those challenges. *Look Up and Beyond* is also a useful tool for educators and mentors to utilize and share with their students. This is a book that will not only help and inspire students, but it will also motivate and impact communities." ~ *Raymond Ramos, Former NYPD Detective & Founder/ CEO Project HYPE (Helping Young People Evolve, Inc)*

"As a college administrator, I have worked with thousands of students over the years from all walks of life. In my experience, what always seems to separate the truly successful ones from the rest is their ability to persist in the face of adversity—and to know they are not alone in their struggle. With heartfelt stories and direct strategies, this book offers both to the reader; Jessica speaks right to the heart of the matter and offers a pathway to persistence everyone can follow. *Definitely*, add it to your library of tools for student success!" ~ *Denise Dellaporta, Student Life Specialist for Peer Mentoring, Leadership & Success, Borough of Manhattan Community College*

"I have an extensive background working with adolescents and adults who are the product of being raised by the criminal justice system. I have witnessed the outcome of unresolved emotional and mental issues. I see the devastating effects of exposure to violence, crime, unhealthy relationships, trauma, lack of positive leadership and loss of hope. Sadly, today's youth live a life where the risk factors by far outweigh the protective factors. I believe that the two most valuable treasures one can be gifted are the gift of hope and education. Education teaches a better way, where hope encourages and motivates the learner to apply what's been learned. I believe that the honest and transparent content of this read will change the nation one life at a time, one family at a time, one community at a time. Jessica is more than an author; she is an example, a living testimony of what one can accomplish in life if they are open to learning, applying, and Looking Up and Beyond!" ~ *Evangeline Snell, Social Worker & Youth Advocate, Friends of Island Academy*

"Jessica Janniere's book is the mentor, friend, and older sister I wish I had as a teenager! *Look Up and Beyond* is an essential read for any student who wants to achieve more, succeed more, and recognize their worth. Jessica gives us relatable, funny, vulnerable, and real stories on the struggles and joys of growing up, dealing with your past, and creating your future place in the world. You will be moved by her journal entries, and you will walk away from this book believing you're worth it, you matter, and your best days are ahead of you." ~ *Bert Gervais aka "The Mentor Guy", Author & Founder of Success Mentor Education*

"The book, *Look Up and Beyond*, is extremely relevant for all ages, but is most notably useful for today's youth as the strategic principles outlined in every chapter help the young (and young at heart!) tackle very real issues that they might experience on a daily basis. *Look Up and Beyond* also details innovative methods for educational institutions to address socio-emotional learning and incorporate literacy into their character development curriculum to ensure that students become leaders of their own lives. This is a must-read book that will not only leave you feeling intrigued, but also inspire and motivate you to look far beyond your adversity!" ~ *Rhonda G. Antoine, Educator and Doctoral Candidate*

"Jessica's book gives an intimate view of her life not for the purpose of vanity but for the purpose of the reader's victory. As someone who speaks to thousands of students a year, I can honestly say they need to read Jessica's book. Life is often disappointing, challenging, and unfair, but Jessica's book will give students the tools and the mindset necessary to overcome all of the challenges they will face." ~ *Odell A. Bizzell II, National Inspirational Storyteller & College Speaker*

"Jessica Janniere's *Look Up and Beyond: Effective Strategies To Become Resilient, Overcome Adversity And Create A Powerful Future* uses reflections from her personal journal as a segue into sections that call young people to develop a mindset of having a clear vision and driving to it without compromise. It provides an avenue for introspection toward self-enhancement and empowerment by deliberately encouraging the reader to animate their actions and action plan and make them manageable in responses to prompts through the book. Models help the reader accomplish this process, and the very process of making thoughts tangible is itself healing. This book, taken seriously, can help any young person navigate the road called Life." ~ *Karlene Jackson Thompson, Assistant Dean of Students, Division of Campus Life, LIU Brooklyn*

"*Look Up and Beyond* is a burst of positive energy and concrete strategies for anyone! All of us have our struggles, some more than others, but they are very real to every individual and the emotions and self-talk attached to those experiences can be so detrimental to our success. This book provides the reader with a wealth of validation and positive affirmations to help us move beyond the negative experiences and the internal barriers we create as a result. I appreciate the brevity of each section, providing just enough relatable information, then delving right into the positive strategies we can use to help us reach our full potential. It does a great job of reframing struggle, adversity, and trauma as experiences that help build and guide us, even providing us with tools and strengths we would not otherwise have. Look Up and Beyond is a positive tool for success in a society currently struggling with a lot of negativity. I highly recommend this book." ~ *Nina Stemm, LMFT-GEAR UP District Coordinator for Vancouver Public Schools and Licensed Marriage Family Therapist.*

"Just reading the first few pages made me wish that someone had written such a book when I was a young person searching for answers to my many questions. Jessica transparently shares how she allowed her pain to transform her and lead her to her purpose. A must-read for anyone working with students." ~ *Renee Crump-Dedmon, Former NYC School Principal*

This book is dedicated
to every young person
who is *fighting* to see beyond
the storms of life.

Hang on.

After darkness, comes sunlight.
After sadness, comes joy.
And after pain, comes purpose.

It is also dedicated to the memory of my sister,
RIP *Viktoria Nadja Thomas*

Nov. 27th, 1982 – Nov. 26th, 1998

Time hasn't removed the pain.

I've only learned to cope with it in a healthy way.

Miss you beyond words.

Table of Contents

Foreword

There are few books you pick up that you realize have the ability to radically change the course of someone's life. When I first read the book, you hold in your hands, I realized at a very deep level that our adversity can actually be our advantage.

As someone who grew up in the projects of Brooklyn, NY, I was well aware of how a traumatic past can infringe on a bright future. I witnessed friends get murdered, imprisoned, and unfortunately give up at a young age.

This book shows how anyone, no matter what kind of troubling and negative background they have, they can create an exciting vision for the future that changes the actions one takes today.

"Look Up and Beyond" is not just the title of this book but a mantra for success. Our past doesn't define us; we define our past. This idea can allow for any situation to go from overwhelming to overcame.

Though time travel doesn't exist, and none of us can go back in time to change our past, this book shows you how to change the meaning you give to the past so that it can serve as your fuel instead of your frustration.

When you read this book and apply the principles within it, you should get a sense of meaning. Meaning creates happiness.

With the unfortunate rise of depression, anxiety, and many other mental health challenges, this book provides practical trauma-informed care for anyone experiencing a tough circumstance or for someone looking to help someone they know who is going through challenges. This will be the book every counselor, parent, mentor, and teacher will want to have in their utility belt to affect positive change in others.

Most importantly, the messenger of this book, Jessica Janniere, doesn't approach overcoming trauma from some ivory tower.

She lives it. She embodies it. And she absolutely understands it.

If you are looking for a book to get you unstuck from the chains of the past and give you a new-found sense of freedom for who you really are and who you can become, you now hold the blueprint to real success in your hands.

Read every word of this book, but most importantly, apply it!

May you experience what it is to look up and beyond a negative past and create a powerful future.

You. Are. Awesome!

-Arel Moodie

Founder of the College Success Program & host of the iTunes top career podcast The Art of Likability

Preface

This book Look Up and Beyond (Student Edition) is unique in the way it is written, but it is going to give you what you need to change your life *forever*. It will help you deal with the tough times you may be facing now or in the future so that you can still have the hope you need to gain a vision for your life. Having a vision for your life is the single most important component to living a successful life—as a student and beyond.

It doesn't matter where you come from, what your circumstances are, what happened in your past, or what you have or don't have. After reading this book, you will be equipped to be a finisher. You will finish the goals you set out to meet. You will finish the projects you start. You will finish each step towards your educational goals. And one day, when you reach the end of your life, someone will say you finished well. You will be remembered because you will have applied the skills I teach you in this book.

I want you to be who you were born to be—and that is more than you can imagine right now. Know this: God doesn't make junk. You are filled with endless possibilities of great things to contribute to this world. **You are here for a purpose.**

I know that the journey to becoming that person won't be easy. Truth be told, it's going to be very tough. Life is filled with storms, those negative things that bring tears. Adversity is part of life, inside and outside of school, and you will need to be resilient to live out your potential and your purpose. There are three different phases we encounter with storms: 1) Getting ready to enter a storm 2) Currently in a storm 3) Just getting out of a storm.

I want you to identify where you are in those three phases

because what I know about life is that we are always in one of those stages.

The truth is I also wrote this book for students who feel like their whole life has been a storm. It seems like, even in your youth, that life is burdensome, unfulfilling, painful, and unfair.

Bad things happen to good people. I had a lot of bad things happen to me. I share some of my stories throughout the book at the beginning of each chapter. You will see that many of those things were out of my control, and I was a victim of my circumstances. But, once aware of my power, I chose to move from victim to victor! You can too!

There may be things—bad things—happening to you or around you that you have no control of. It's tough, I know, but as I learned we are not defined by those things. You are not what happened to you.

You can look up and hold your head high with confidence knowing that you are stronger than you think; you are valuable and powerful. You can start to think, dream, and plan for a better future. And, you can take the bad things that happened to you and use them as stepping stones to discover your potential and beyond.

When you complete this book, you will have the tools you need to be resilient or to bounce back from every setback and disappointment in your life. You will have a vision of your future, and it will be the energy source that keeps you going forth, no matter the storms you face.

That's what *Look Up and Beyond* is all about. It's more than a phrase. **It's a mindset, a lifestyle, and a global movement.**

Getting the Most Out of This Book

This book was uniquely written to inspire you to look up and beyond where you currently are while equipping you to get to where you want to be.

Here's the thing: You MUST get engaged. No one can read this book for you-you must do it for YOU.

In the beginning of every chapter, you will see a **positive quote** to motivate you. I suggest you begin collecting quotes that resonate with you, quotes that really touch your heart and make you feel hopeful and encouraged. You can refer to them anytime for inspiration while on your journey.

Every chapter opens with "**From My Journal.**" These journal entries were used to publish my memoir, *My Colored World*. These stories give you a sense of the tough times I had to overcome. Some of my stories are very personal. I want you to see that I am not coming to tell you to do something that I personally have not done. I want you to see that my life hasn't always been easy, and I've had some unfair and painful things happen to me. There were times in my life that I didn't think I could make it beyond my pain, but with faith and perseverance, I did.

I was able to learn the strategies that I teach you in this book. I've taught them to countless students and young people—including my own kids. These strategies are the things I wish I knew when I was your age. I didn't have anyone to teach me then, but after surviving these situations, I am not only thriving but living a life that inspires and equips people from all over the world to look up and BEYOND.

I encourage you to purchase a journal just for writing beyond the space in this book. That is engagement, and *it will change your life*. I promise. My journals were and continue to be a place of venting, healing, reflection, hope, and vision-building. Journaling is one of the most powerful coping strategies we can use to become more resilient.

In each chapter, there is a specific **Look Up and Beyond Strategy** that you can apply immediately. These principles work, but **you** have to work them. Countless successful students from all over the world use these strategies to achieve their goals and biggest dreams. You can too.

Next, there is a **Reflections** section. This part is important because you can write down what you are personally learning from the chapter. Be sure to write down your answers. When you write them down, you are capturing a moment in time that will never be again. Who you are today is not who you're becoming. Capture these moments, and over time, you'll see the growth and success manifest.

The **Goal Getter** section is designed to inspire action. Growth requires action. Take the time to follow through and act.

The **High Achiever Challenge** is for you, the student, who wants to go beyond the average. You believe in going the extra mile because you know it will set you apart from mediocrity. Don't settle for good when you can be great.

You will also notice an affirmation at the end of every chapter. When we affirm something, we are proclaiming that it is so. **Affirmations** are a powerful tool you can use to encourage yourself.

We can't always depend on others to build us up; we all have to take personal responsibility for ourselves. Speaking affirmations out loud is a way to do that. So when you get to the end of each chapter, stand up and affirm yourself with confidence and power as you speak that affirmation.

As you read this book, have fun. Be open-minded. Be introspective. Be honest. Be involved.

"Life becomes easier when you learn to accept the apology you never got."

~ Robert Brault

I am so sorry.

I know you're probably reading this and wondering, "Why are you saying sorry when you don't even know me and didn't do anything to me?" That may be true, but hear this:

I'm sorry.

I'm sorry for the times you were bullied and hurt. I'm sorry for the times you were neglected and overlooked. I'm sorry for the times that unfair things happened to you that you can't understand. I'm sorry that at times, life is painful, unfair, and discouraging.

I am here not on behalf of the person who hurt you. I am here because I've been where you are: trying to get past toxic people and storms in my life. I want to be the one who apologizes to you for the things that happened to you because maybe the person who *should've* apologized, *didn't*.

I'm sorry for your pain.

I hope you'll accept this apology.

I. Embrace Your Uniqueness

"Today you are you! That is truer than true! There is no one alive who is you-er than you!" ~ Dr. Seuss

From My Journal: *Coming to America* (Age 6)

Sitting in the back of the car, I began to get very restless, constantly turning around to sit on my knees so I could look out of the back window. I saw a lot of movement. I felt tense. My mind was confused. My spirit felt heavy, and my stomach ached terribly. As my step-father, Elmont, jumped into the driver's seat, slamming the door behind him, my heart dropped. My mother quickly followed him and jumped into the seat beside him. Once her door slammed shut, I began to weep. It seemed like my entire life was shattering. I didn't know much, but what I did know was enough to scare me.

My mother and step-father had this all planned out, I thought, leaving Germany to come to America. Just like that. "I don't even know this man. I don't trust him," I said to myself. As the car started, I hurt even more. The tears began to stream endlessly down my face. I watched out the back of the car window as Oma stood in front of the house, slowly waving goodbye. I watched, and I wept. She got smaller and smaller in the distance until I no longer saw her.

I had just experienced one of my deepest heartbreaks at the tender age of six. Life was showing its cruel side.

You see, my life had been filled with innocence and overwhelming love and adoration. Growing up on a farm in Tiefenbach Germany, I clearly remember the joy of working with my Oma and Opa (Grandma and Grandpa) as we pulled vegetables and fruits out of the dirt in the garden. Opa would take me into the barn to play on the hay and allowed me to be his number one spectator as he slaughtered the pigs. Oma was the closest thing I had to a mom. She lovingly received me, an underweight baby girl, when my mom just dropped me off at her doorstep like I was a package of supplies. She had nowhere to turn, so she turned to Oma. I lived with Oma for the first six years of my life.

During that time, my mom met a black soldier named Elmont. He was tall and slim and had a smooth Jeri curl and hazel eyes. All the German women loved him because he seemed so mysterious, so charming. His seemingly quiet and calm demeanor was something my mom was attracted to. They hooked up, and she got pregnant with my half-sister, Vicky, which caused a big stir in a small white town. This small town was already filled with hatred toward blacks, so when everyone heard the news about Eva giving birth to a biracial child, the racist remarks became louder and heavier. Mom and Elmont got married at town hall the next year with military approval.

Through those times, I still lived with Oma, unaware of the struggles. For me, life was innocent until…it was time to go to America.

As I sat in the car headed to Frankfurt Airport, I felt like my mother had just died. I didn't know how to handle the pain inside me. I hurt. I felt confused. Why was this woman taking me away from my home? As these thoughts ran through my mind, I yearned for a hug and a warm touch. Instead, I got silence and isolation. I don't remember much of what happened after that. All I knew is that we were headed to America.

Look Up and Beyond Strategy #1: Embrace Your Uniqueness

The dictionary states that the word **unique** means "being the only one of its kind; unlike anything else. A unique person or thing." The dictionary is talking about **YOU**!

There is only ONE you. Everything about you is different from anyone else. Your fingerprint is an indication of this fact.

Most times, when we think about fingerprints, we think about them in a negative way. Have you ever watched a movie or TV show that had a crime theme? If so, most likely when the suspect is apprehended, law enforcement takes them into a room and takes their mugshot, then their fingerprints. According to Encyclopedia.com, here's why:

"Fingerprint evidence is seen as one of the best types of physical evidence linking a suspect to an object or location or for establishing identity. Therefore, the forensic investigator will always search for fingerprint evidence at the scene of a crime and at related locations, such as a suspect's home or car. A fingerprint is the pattern of ridges and related characteristics found on the finger pads, the fleshy parts of the fingers used for touching and gripping. Each person's fingerprints are unique and stay unchanged throughout life. According to Sir Francis Galton, the nineteenth-century English anthropologist, the chances of two fingerprints being identical are as small as 64 billion to one. In over a century of forensic fingerprinting, no two prints have ever been found to be the same, even those of identical twins."

Your fingerprint metaphorically tells you that whatever you touch and create, **no one** can do it the way you do. It serves as a reminder that you are different and that is not only okay, but it's GOOD.

Think about it this way: Whether you want to pursue politics, healthcare, engineering, or aviation, there may be countless other people who have held positions in those respective fields. But, no one was you. And looking forward, no one **is** you. So when you step into your position, even though it may be similar in title and responsibility to someone else, no one can fulfill it like you. Beyond skills—which anyone can learn with focus, discipline and time—you bring something unique to the table: your personality, your life experience, and your fingerprint.

Everything about you is unique.

When I was younger, I hated my story. I never talked about it. I was embarrassed by it. But what's so interesting is that my story is what connects me to my purpose. My story, in all its uniqueness, makes me who I am today.

I was born in a small German town and lived on a farm for the first six years of my life. One day, my life drastically changed. I became a step-child and half-sibling in a family that had a lot of abuse and dysfunction. On top of that, the area I grew up in was poor, crime-ridden, and predominantly black. I stood out everywhere I went and couldn't fit in anywhere. I became a target for bullying and developed a sense of self-hate and shame.

I wanted to keep my story a secret.

But, I learned that our stories and experiences play a part in shaping us—and that is important. Just as you are unique as an individual, so is your story. Today, I embrace my unique story. I tell my story unashamedly. This is what makes me able to connect with people from all different walks of life. It wasn't until I embraced my uniqueness that I was able to fully discover my potential and purpose.

Different is positive. **Different is powerful.** Embrace your uniqueness and discover the power you possess because of it.

REFLECTION: Besides your fingerprint, what are some unique qualities about you? Do you see them as a negative or positive? Why?

_____

_____

_____

_____

_____

_____

_____

_____

_____

GO GETTER GOAL: After reading this chapter, what unique qualities about yourself will you embrace and own more? What personal affirmations can you create using those qualities? What will you do to ensure you affirm yourself daily?

_____

_____

_____

_____

_____

_____

_____

_____

_____

_____

HIGH ACHIEVER CHALLENGE: How can you appreciate not only your uniqueness, but the uniqueness others have? What are some simple yet powerful things you can do to express to others that you accept them and their uniqueness?

_____

_____

_____

_____

_____

_____

_____

_____

_____

AFFIRMATION:
"I am powerfully unique!"

II. Believe You Are Valuable

"Make sure you don't see yourself through the eyes of those who don't value you. Know your worth; even if they don't." ~ Jessica Janniere

From My Journal: *Father's Day Card* (Age 8)

I was in class with Ms. Levine, my third-grade teacher. She was a tall, slim, and stylish white woman. She had very short, blonde, dramatic hair and wore a lot of makeup. As a class project, we had to make Father's Day cards in the shape of a tie. Well, I was certain that I could make the best one and that Elmont would finally see how much I loved him. I cut along the lines of my traced tie. I then colored it blue and bronze. I added some black to make it look "manly."

I was proud of my tie. I even wrote a short note on the inside that said, "Dear Dad, I love you and I want to be a good girl. I hope you will love this tie. I made it just for you, Jessica." I couldn't wait until Sunday. That Sunday I woke up with great anticipation and excitement. Today would be the day. It would all change. I would get my step-father to see that I am his daughter and that I love him. He will see that I want him to be my Dad. He's the only "Dad" I've ever known. "There's a reason for this," I thought. God planned it this way. He'll get it today.

Reality hit me. I didn't know how to give this card to him. I felt overwhelmed. I was trying to plan it out in my mind. How could I not think about this before? I walked around, restless, trying to watch for the right moment to place it on his side of the bed. Maybe on top of the nightstand. I noticed he had left the room and went to the bathroom. This was my chance. I quickly went to get the card. I ran to his "forbidden" side of the bed and laid the card on top of the nightstand. He couldn't miss it.

I ran out of the room quickly, my heart racing. My thoughts were running a thousand miles per hour with images of his reaction. I sat around in the living room, which was attached to a small hallway section that led to his room. He walked past me and went back to his spot on the end of the bed. He sat there and watched TV, sipping his beer. It seemed like forever before he turned around to even notice the special something on his nightstand. I watched from the living room as he stretched his arm out to grab the card and slowly walked towards the bedroom.

I knew this would be the moment where he would hug me and tell me he was sorry for misunderstanding me. As I entered the doorway, his back was turned to me. He didn't know I was standing there. I saw him look at the card, quickly flip it over, and then tear it up. Yes, he tore it up and threw it into the garbage pail beside his bed. He casually looked back and saw me, then simply turned back to the TV, shaking his head. He grabbed his 40oz. malt liquor and took another sip. I ran away to my room and wept.

My world was crushed. I was so confused. I hated him, and I hated myself. I felt like my heart was torn up with the card. I started to think that if my skin was darker, he would accept me. I decided that day that I would never make another card for him or anyone else. I felt the anger simmer deep within me. My heart hardened some more.

Look Up and Beyond Strategy #2: Believe That You Are Valuable

You are living now, in this place, in the world, on purpose. There is something inside of you that only you can bring to the world. Your life is a mosaic of experiences threaded together over time to create this beautiful picture of YOU. And guess what? You are capable of more than you can even imagine. You are valuable. You may not feel like you are, but feelings can lie to us sometimes.

Your value is not dependent on other people and situations. Your value is not even dependent on your accomplishments. Many of us are taught that when we accomplish goals like making honor roll, winning a championship, or getting voted for to be class president, that we are somehow more important than those students who are failing classes and getting in trouble. That's not true. Circumstances don't dictate the value of a person.

Some of us are taught that our looks determine our value. If someone is attractive, they're usually more popular, so we believe that they are more important—more valuable. That is also not true. Value is not determined by outside sources but by the very creation of you. I believe in God (I'm not telling you what to believe) and that He created us ALL with a purpose. The very creation of you makes you valuable.

I wish I knew that the day my step-father ripped up that Father's Day card. When he rejected my card, I took it as a sure sign that I was a nobody. The pain of rejection made me feel that I was not valuable and shaped my self-image in a negative way for many years. I was very self-destructive because of that rejection. I thought that Elmont's response to me was a calculation of my value. Gosh, was I wrong.

There is a big difference between our value and the experiences that we encounter in our lives that may make us feel that we are not valuable. Here's what I mean by that:

Let's say, you were abused, and because of that abuse, you feel worthless. Well, the abuse cannot take your value away. Your perspective about the abuse limits you from seeing your value. The abuse, although it is wrong—and I wish it didn't happen to you—does not have the power to decrease your value as a person. You are still valuable. You still have a purpose. There is still something that you were born to do in a way that only YOU can do it. Unfortunately, you experienced something negative and painful that will challenge your belief about that.

You will need time to heal from bad experiences that happen, and the healing process is different for everyone, but regardless of the healing journey you embark on, you start at an important place, a place of incredible value. YOU are valuable. Nothing that happened to you, or will happen to you, can ever change that.

Once you recognize and embrace your unique value, you become stronger and better.

Look at it this way:

I take a $100 bill out of my pocket. (I don't carry those with me just in case you're wondering.) Then I take the $100 bill, rip it in half, throw it on the floor, step on it, pick it up, crumble it in my hand and throw it back down on the floor and leave it there. What is that $100 worth now? $100. Sure, I'll have to piece it back together again, but its value is still there. Regardless of my treatment towards the bill, the $100 bill is still worth $100.

My point is this:

You have to look up and beyond all the bad things that have happened to you and see your value. It was threaded into your being when God created you. That didn't and won't ever change.

You just gotta believe it.

If you are struggling to see your worth and value, get around people who will see it and remind you of it often. Check out the chapter entitled "Select Your Squad Carefully." I teach you how to be intentional about the relationships in your life. You are valuable, and only people who see that and treat you in that way deserve to be in your space, and it's important that the people you choose to surround yourself with are adding value to you.

I believe in you, and without even knowing you, I know this about you: you are valuable.

REFLECTION: Do you believe that you are a valuable person? Why or why not? What are some of the negative things that happened to you that make you feel you are not valuable?

_____

_____

_____

_____

_____

_____

_____

_____

GO GETTER GOAL: Write down everything you think about what makes YOU valuable. Turn your answers into personal affirmations to speak to yourself daily.

_____

_____

_____

_____

_____

_____

_____

_____

_____

HIGH ACHIEVER CHALLENGE: What are some of the things you can do to heal yourself from past painful events? Who can you reach out to for support?

_____

_____

_____

_____

_____

_____

_____

_____

_____

AFFIRMATION:

"I am valuable!"

III. Focus on What You Can Control

"It's not where you start – it's where you finish that counts." ~ Zig Ziglar

From My Journal: *Nothing Ever Changed* (Age 9)

I was at my new school now. It was just a walk down the block and around the corner. Although so close, the daily walk seemed like miles. Especially when a group of local kids rallied behind me, cursing and looking for a fight. It was always a big neighborhood fiasco. Getting to and from school was more like being in a TV episode of "Survivor." By this time, I was starting to learn that I had to hit back and I had to hit hard. Pain was the name of the game. It was ruthless. It didn't quit. But at times, I felt like quitting.

The big school building stood surrounded by a big yard and two playgrounds. The grass hills leading up to the back entrance of the school looked so picturesque. Behind the walls of the building was a nightmare waiting for me. As I left home each morning, I had just left a nightmare, then I went to school and walked right into another. I would sit in class trying to concentrate on my work, and it was so hard. Sometimes, I was hurting from the welts on my body. Then, there were days when my stomach ached from hunger. Food was low, and Mom was too stressed to make sure we ate.

On any particular day, hurtful words were yelled at me on my way out the door; it served as a reminder of how unworthy of love I was. As I sat at my desk, spitballs hit the back of my neck. I tried to ignore it as I heard snickers and words like "honky" and "white bread" in the midst of the soft voices. "Get her in her long giraffe neck. Get that white honky." It seemed like each time I looked back to see who was spitting the balls my way, I would get caught and yelled at. I was embarrassed as the teacher shouted, "Why can't you sit still? Get out into the hallway… now!" I burst into tears and angrily ran out the class door.

The symphony of laughter echoed in the background. I leaned on the hallway wall with tears streaming down. I began to bang my fist and head on the hard brick wall. I screamed out, "I want to die. I hate everyone. I hate life. I hate myself." My teacher looked at me in confusion and pity. I hated her too. She didn't know what my life was like. How dare she have pity on me? And how dare she embarrass me like that? She sent me to the guidance counselor's office, and I sat there the rest of the day feeling defeated.

Many days were spent in that office from that point on. I started to enjoy the one-on-one attention from Mr. Nicholson. He was a tall, slinky, white guy with dark hair who always seemed to wear the same clothes every day: a black suit with a white shirt and black bowtie. When I think back, he was nerdy looking and reminded me of Pee Wee Herman. I liked that he listened to me, and I began to open up to him about what was happening in my life.

He was the first person I told about the various forms of punishment I had to endure at home. I shared how I had to stand in the corner of a room facing the wall. I had to stand there for hours and could not lean on the wall despite my exhaustion. Most nights, Elmont and the rest of the family were snuggled in bed, and I had to stay awake into the morning. He would randomly pop into the room to make sure I was standing as he instructed. When I dozed off or leaned on the wall and he found out, all hell broke loose. Those times, my mom would start screaming and crying, begging him to stop. Then, he'd beat her and me. When my siblings woke up, he calmly told them to go back to bed.

As I shared, Mr. Nicholson listened attentively. As he listened, he gave me thick salted pretzel sticks he kept in his office that

I would snack on between our talks. I was filled with so many emotions, and he gave me an outlet. After a few sessions, I began to show him the bruises on my body that my clothes hid; the black and blues, welts, and open bloody cuts. Sometimes, they were from a "switch," a thin flexible, yet strong wooden stick. Other times, Elmont used an extension cord or clothes hanger. Regardless of what he used, I was left with deep welts and an aching back and bottom. Sometimes, I'd bleed. Sitting hurt. Walking hurt. And if I had to fight at school, it was pain on top of pain. He called in the school nurse who examined me, and they looked at each other in horror.

I was afraid. I didn't want to get my family in trouble, but I was angry. My young mind and heartfelt overwhelmed. Before long, the principal came and a lady they said was a social worker. The lady told me that they would interview my mom and stepfather. Now, I was even more afraid. If Elmont found out that I told on him, he would kill me for sure. My stomach ached. On the day of the interview, Elmont made sure I stayed in my room. He lied about everything, and they believed him. Nothing ever changed.

Look Up and Beyond Strategy #3: Focus on What You CAN Control

There is nothing more frustrating than **wanting** to change a negative situation or person that you have **no control** over. It is emotionally and mentally draining when we focus our energies on things we can't control. It is much wiser to shift that energy to something we CAN control. And listen, the ONLY thing you have control over is YOU! You control how you respond or don't respond and what you choose to do with your circumstances— good or bad.

That day when the social worker came to our house, she did not help me the way I thought she would. As disappointed as I was, I believe it was one of the defining moments that showed me - sometimes, there are things we truly have no control over. I was a child when the abuse happened. And abuse is never okay.

It should not have happened, but it did.

As I look back, I wish I would've kept asking for help. But I didn't. I lost my voice and felt defeated. Years later, I had to make a decision. Would I become and stay bitter or would I become better? I decided to become better.

Most people get bitter when bad things happen to them, but not you; you will get better. Stronger. Tougher. And you will be more successful as a student and person overall. The truth is you only have control of two things in any given situation. First is your attitude towards it, and second is your action towards it.

The way to step into your power and become a student who is in control of what you can control is to take full responsibility for your life. This means that you recognize and accept that your parents, your teachers, your peers, your mentors, or anyone else is not responsible for you; you are.

When you take full responsibility for your life, you activate your inner power. You are also stating that you will not be a victim to the bad things that may have happened to you. When you take full responsibility for yourself, you are empowering yourself to walk into your future like a boss. You will be much more excited about life and feel more joy than you can imagine.

One of the most important aspects of this principle is choosing your attitude. A negative attitude will never give us a positive life. We must decide to have a positive attitude. Our attitude determines our altitude, or how high we will go in life. Our attitudes attract or detract success in our lives.

Decide today that you will *choose* to have a positive attitude no matter what is going on in your life.

It is very difficult to develop a positive attitude when you live in a negative environment, but it is not impossible. You will need a strong determination, focus, and a strategic plan to develop conscious positive self-talk.

I've learned a few strategies that will empower you to live above and beyond any negativity in your life. Check them out:

A good attitude starts with a good mind. Monitor your

thoughts and take notice when you're thinking negatively.

Replace negative thoughts with positive ones. Be intentional and consistent. Here's an example of how to do this:

Let's say you're sitting in a classroom waiting to take a test. While you're waiting for your exam, you start to think "I'm going to fail this. I'm so dumb. I don't know this subject. I didn't study." Instead, make a conscious effort to think "I'm going to give this test my best. I am capable. I am going to put my best foot forward. I will study more next time. Hey, maybe I can discuss this with my teacher to see if I can retake the test if I don't do so well."

Our minds are like computers. They download information from our environment constantly. There are some things we have no control of in our environment, but when we do, we should be wise and use that opportunity to create a positive environment.

If you live in a dysfunctional home (maybe noisy, chaotic, emotionally draining, etc.), but you have your own room, you can create a positive environment in your room. You can post pictures of your dreams on your wall. You can also create a vision board.

Go to YouTube and type **Motivational Videos** in the Search bar. Start browsing and listening to positive and encouraging content. Some of my favorite motivational talks are from John C. Maxwell, Les Brown, and Oprah.

Play music that makes you feel positive. Create a playlist with only positive, motivating, and encouraging songs. Listen to it daily.

Post your affirmations on your wall where you can see them every day. Remember, speak them out loud. This makes them more powerful because your brain hears this and will believe it more and more over time.

If you don't have your own room, you can still create an environment of positivity. It will take more effort, but it will be worth it. Here are a few strategies:

Identify a positive place that you can spend time daily or a few times a week. This could be in your guidance counselor's office, after school in a teacher's classroom, at an organization that will allow you an opportunity to volunteer for them, a student club, or a sports team.

Keep positive quotes and expressions everywhere you go. Put them on your phone, tablet—basically any electronic device you use—notebooks, keychains, lockers, etc.

A positive attitude will make you more resilient. It will change your perspective about you, other people, your environment, and the challenges you may face. Remember, along with your attitude, focus on the things you CAN control. Doing so activates your power, and you will feel great, your confidence will increase, and ultimately, you will attract success in school and beyond.

REFLECTION: Think about the most positive person you know. How do you feel when you're around them? What do notice most about them? _____

_____

_____

_____

_____

_____

_____

_____

GO GETTER GOAL: What are some specific things you can do to take control of your life?

_____

_____

_____

_____

_____
_____
_____
_____
_____

HIGH ACHIEVER CHALLENGE: What specific steps are you willing to take to ensure that you have a positive attitude?

_____
_____
_____
_____
_____
_____
_____
_____

AFFIRMATION:

"I am responsible for me and my future!"

IV. Get and Cultivate a Vision for Your Life

> "The only thing worse than being blind is having
> sight but no vision."
> ~ Helen Keller

From My Journal: *Bottles & Cans* (Age 11)

One cold day, my Mom and I were talking through the streets in our town. We fought the harsh winds as we picked up empty bottles and cans we found lying on the ground or in someone's garbage can. I didn't have a warm coat, so my body hungered for warmth. I started counting the bottles we already had, to keep my mind off the cold.

Tears of frustration and shame fell. Even though I was cold, I was trying to help her. I felt so low, so hopeless. I felt so ashamed that we had to resort to this. I hated her for asking me to come with her. I didn't want to do this. I saw the sadness in her eyes as she looked through some of the garbage cans, rummaging through them in hope of finding a bottle, a can —anything of value.

I'm sure she felt bad that I was out there, but I didn't feel her concern. I felt too angry with her. I hated her. I hated that she loved Elmont. I hated that she was afraid of him. I hated that she was weak. "I will never be weak. I will never rely on some man or person to help me," I kept saying to myself. "I'm gonna go and be rich one day."

Looking back now, I know she why was so afraid; she was afraid of being abandoned with five kids to care for. No valuable job skills. No family support. Not good at speaking English. It seemed like an even more hopeless situation without Elmont around.

As we took the big garbage bags filled with the bottles and cans to the grocery store, I dreaded having to stand there by the machine as people walked by. All I needed was another kid from around the way see me putting them in the machine. My stomach knotted up as I played out different scenarios of different people walking by seeing me and my mom "being poor."

This was a life of constant struggle. We were consumed with the preoccupation of just trying to survive. In the hood, we knew we only had that moment. The rest of the day wasn't guaranteed. Anything past then didn't matter. It was minute by minute, hour by hour, and day by day.

That day will forever be embedded in my memory as a painful day, but I am glad for that day. It inspired me to search beyond my circumstances. It was at that moment I knew that I didn't know what I wanted, but I did know what I didn't want. Knowing what I did NOT want helped me cultivate a vision for my life.

Look Up and Beyond Strategy #4: Get and Cultivate a Vision for Your Life

It is so important to have a vision for your life. What is a vision? A vision is when you have a picture in your mind of what you want your future to look like. Having a vision is important because if you are in a situation where you're going through a tough time or your circumstances are not what you would like them to be, your vision will give you something to look forward to and work towards.

When I was growing up, it seemed like I could never catch a break. Life was always kind of dark, gloomy, and stressful. I had to find ways to "see" beyond my now. Along with reading books to get my mind off the stress, along with volunteering and making sure that I was out of the house to do positive things, I thought up a vision and held onto it.

Now, I did go through times in my life where I felt hopeless and wanted to quit. I realized years later that I simply didn't have the right strategies to cope with the stress in a good and healthy way. That is one of the reasons I wrote this book; I want YOU to have these strategies early in life so you don't go through life making avoidable mistakes or be defined by your failures and heartbreak.

I believed that life had to be better than what I was living through each day, that there had to be some positive experiences after these storms passed, and I began to dream. I'm a big dreamer. Even to this day, I dream. I dream a lot, and if you're a daydreamer, you're powerful; every great invention and movement started as a dream. Dreamers are powerful. Don't let anybody tell you, "Oh, stop dreaming," or, "Stop daydreaming." (Unless of course you're in school and your daydreaming is interfering with your ability to focus in class. Then, you need to get focused on being present and participating.)

When you have a dream, your dream is usually tied to a vision that is planted in your heart. When you have a vision and you nurture it by being intentional about pursuing it, it will energize you. It will keep you motivated. It will bring you hope. It will keep you going during difficult times. Having a vision will help you look up and beyond everything that you're going through so you can have this idea and belief that, "I may be going through a tough time now, and things may seem a little shaky and uncertain, but my best is yet to come. What's coming is going to be better."

A vision empowers you to begin to think about who you are going to be in the future. Think about this: Where do you see your life going in the next three years, five years, and ten years? What will you want to have accomplished by then? What schools and colleges do you envision attending? What awards do you see yourself getting? Where do you want to live? What experiences do you want to live in the years ahead of you? What kind of work do you want to be doing in your career? How will you be of positive service to your family, community, and country?

We all need to have a vision; without a vision, we literally perish. We become hopeless. We stop dreaming, and we can't see beyond the day to day life, which is a place of survival for many people. I know what that's like, but I learned that we were not born to just survive from day to day. We were born to thrive. Having a vision will inspire you to thrive.

Think about the future you want to have. What vision do you have in your mind? What is sitting on your heart and comes up often? What dreams do you have? You may be the only person in your family to ever attempt to do these things. That's okay. If you can dream it and envision it, it's possible. You have to believe that it's possible. If you don't believe that it's possible, you have to get around people who will believe it for you. That way, you can find strength in and borrow their belief.

As mentioned previously, one of the things that I used to do in my youth is journal—a lot. That is one of the reasons I created the *Reflections, Goal-Getting,* and *High Achiever* sections in this book. I created these sections to encourage you to write down your thoughts and your ideas. In my journals, I would vent and share my pains, my frustrations, and my disappointments. I talked about the things that hurt me, but I also talked about my dreams: my dreams to be loved and to be cared for, to be respected, to accomplish something great in life, and to change the world.

I didn't know how I was going to do it, and to be honest with you, there was a large part of me that didn't know if it was even possible, but I kept dreaming, and I kept going back to this vision. I also had people around me that believed in me more than I believed in myself. They helped me find the courage to move forward despite the adversity in my life.

But no adversity can stop someone who has a vision and is committed to seeing it unfold. When you hold onto a vision that you can become passionate about, the situations and the people that you need to help fulfill the vision also begin to come into your life. You literally become a magnet. You start to attract people who believe in you, sometimes more than you believe in yourself, and they will push you forward. They'll open up a door of opportunity for you to get closer to that vision becoming a reality, but it's your responsibility to hold onto that vision.

Again, who do you see yourself becoming in the next few years? Do you see yourself graduating and holding that diploma? Can you feel the emotion of what that accomplishment feels like after everybody told you that you couldn't, or people doubted you and counted you out?

I was counted out throughout my youth. Because of the people around me, I often questioned if I would be successful. The statistics showed that based on my environment I was growing up in, I'd fail. I was raised on welfare in the hood. I was physically abused in and outside of the home. Statistics showed that I would most likely end up a drug addict, in jail, or even dead.

I almost died a statistic, but I lived to tell about it and have overcome the odds by the grace of God.

I'm here to tell you that I always had a vision, and it played such a major part in helping me to overcome everything I've been through. Yes, it got a little cloudy in some seasons of my life. Yes, I stopped believing sometimes. However, there was always a vision waiting for me to come back to it. I wrote it down. I kept dreaming. I never stopped reading, learning, or growing. If you do the same, you will not just survive, but you'll thrive. You will overcome **anything** including statistics when they're stacked against you.

Get a vision for your life.

REFLECTION: Do you have a vision for your life? What does your future self-look like? Explain in detail how you imagine yourself to be in five and ten years. Write it in present tense as if you are five to ten years older now, writing backwards about your life. You will need extra writing space for this section.

GO GETTER GOAL: Share your vision with someone you trust—a teacher, guidance counselor and/or mentor. Journal their response. You will capture their belief in you for days when you need to be reminded that your dreams and your vision *matter.*

_____

_____

_____

_____

_____

_____

_____

_____

_____

HIGH ACHIEVER CHALLENGE: Google Vision Boards for samples and ideas. Create your own vision board. Hang it up somewhere you can see it daily.

_____

_____

_____

_____

_____

_____

_____

_____

_____

AFFIRMATION:

"I am a visionary!"

V. Select Your Squad Carefully

"If you're looking for a friend, you're going to find they're very scarce. If you go out to be a friend, you'll find them everywhere."
~ Zig Ziglar

From My Journal: _The Unexpected Friend (Age 12)_

It was time to move again. We moved further up on the Peninsula of an area called Far Rockaway, to a large three-family house. We lived on the top floor. The landlord lived on the first floor. They were a West Indian family and were hardly ever around. We had three bedrooms and a nice size living room and kitchen. Elmont made one of the bedrooms the living room. He kept it locked, and no one was allowed to enter. On Fridays, he would come home from work, unlock the living room door, and sit in there as he prepared himself to go out for the weekend. It was almost ritualistic. I knew exactly the time he would come in and go out. I knew he would fix his hair and clothes and blast his music. Michael Jackson was just one of the artists we'd hear over and over and over every week.

On the second floor lived an Irish family. They were just as dysfunctional as we were. The mother of the house drank and smoked cigarettes. She always argued with her husband, and they had a daughter who popped gum. It was annoying. All of them cursed terribly, all day. They owned the towing company across the street from the house. After a while, I got an off-the-books job there. It was cool. I was making some money for myself, and it gave me time away from home.

With the move, it was also time to go to another school. That meant that I would have to go on the bus and again travel further up the Peninsula. That made me very uncomfortable. For one, the kids from the projects attended that school and the high school located directly across the street. Another reason was that there were a lot of white students in the school. I couldn't see myself fitting in even though I was white. Many of them came from the rich area called Belle Harbor. I knew I could never relate to them. I started to hate them before even knowing them.

While I was attending JHS 180, I got into a lot of fights. I was angry and searching for something. I couldn't quite figure it out. If I wasn't skipping school, then I would be in the Dean's office hearing the usual, "Jessica, you gotta try to stay out of trouble." I got caught starting a fire in the bathroom and didn't care that I would face suspension. I cursed out the teachers and even the principal. There was a **deep** anger in me, and I felt that NO ONE could understand me and my challenges, so my attitude was screw them!

I did end up making a friend who helped me through some of my middle school frustrations. She was an unexpected friend. Jenny was a short Puerto Rican girl that walked home from school on the same route I had to take. I started throwing rocks at her and bullying her. For a while, she ignored me, but I kept bothering her, and we got into our little drama-exchanging words. Somewhere in our exchange, we realized we had some things in common. The threats and negative energy over time were replaced with inquisitive talks and good vibes.

Jenny and I ended up becoming best friends the next year. We were now in the same school and same class. We became inseparable those middle school years, and she was part of my exclusive squad.

Look Up And Beyond Strategy #5: Your Squad Matters

My friendship with Jenny was unexpected, but it taught me some things about myself and others. First, I was bullying Jenny because I had anger inside of me that was not expressed properly. The truth is I was hurting, so I hurt others. My own pain was the reason I almost missed the opportunity to have a good friend in my life.

When I think about the friendships I experienced during my youth, I think about two pieces of advice in particular. First, be open to making friends with students who are different from you. Secondly, choose your friends carefully, creating your squad.

Your "squad" is your friends and support circle. Having the right squad is very, very important to your success. Having the right perspective and understanding about relationships with your peers is important as well. There is a lot of power in being connected to people. When we are connected to the wrong people, it works against us. If we're connected to the right people, it works in our favor.

Remember this: you are only in school for a few years. The choices you make today, including the friends you choose, will have an impact on your future—which is not that far away. When you embrace your uniqueness and value, you begin to understand that not everyone can be your "friend." You can be cool with everyone but not chill with them. That means be friendly and respectful to all but selective about who is allowed in your personal space.

You can have countless social media followers and connections, but don't confuse them with friends. You can have people who admire you for whatever reason, but it doesn't mean they are your friends. Genuine friends are extremely hard to find. My advice is: make sure you remember your own worth. Never make your squad selection based on you trying to fill a void. It will put you at risk for dealing with fake friends and future regret.

In high school, I didn't have any friends. I had associates and classmates, but not friends that I can say I was excited about seeing each day. It was lonely at times. Those experiences taught me that there are times when we have to maybe spend some time alone. We're not always going to fit in. We're not always going to be part of a clique. We're not always going to be the popular one, and that's okay. If you are not a popular student and wish you were, learn to be content with your current status.

Popularity is overrated.

Looking back at those years, I realize that a lot of the students who were most popular ended up getting distracted. They had some challenges that could have been avoided had they not been so popular or had they known how to deal with the popularity. The popular students allowed the attention to get to their head, and it became their identity. They also dealt with an overwhelming amount of pressure to constantly be the type of person that their peers wanted them to be. It was a big distraction because, many times, their social life consumed them.

There is nothing wrong with having a vibrant social life or being popular. The important thing is to not look for your identity in it because you won't find it. Doing so puts you at risk for succumbing to all kinds of destructive pressures.

For example, if you are a popular student, there's pressure to always look good and wear the latest styles and name brands. If you, your parents, and guardians can't afford to keep up with your image, you will face the temptation to do whatever it takes to get what you believe you need to keep up with it. That may include stealing, lying, cheating, and more. This does nothing but lead you down a path of destruction. You now face arrest and a legal situation. If you get arrested, you're in the system or in jail, and that stays on your record most of the time. Then, you will have a difficult time finding a job or starting a career. At the end of the day, it's just NOT worth it.

If you're a popular student, make sure you don't allow your popularity to distract from what matters most: your integrity. Integrity is *always* doing the right thing even when it's unpopular. Real friends will NOT put you in a position that compromises your integrity.

If you live for other people's acceptance, you will die from their rejection, and that is giving others TOO much power over you. Remember your uniqueness AND value. It is never based on material things or even other people's opinions.

Sometimes, it is healthy to consider people's opinions. We can learn about ourselves from those close to us. We just want to make sure that the opinions we're accepting and filtering through come from emotionally healthy people. We all need positive people in our lives to help bring out the best in us.

I want to encourage you to get around the students who are doing their best academically, who are involved in student clubs and are moving forward with vision and purpose. They don't see you as competition, but they want to collaborate with you, or they'll just support you. Real friends will encourage you and push you forth. They want to see you win because they know it takes nothing away from them when you win. Be around people that are going to see and bring out the best in you.

We attract who we are. Be the kind of person you want in your life. Or, be the kind of person you wish you had in the past. When we are friendly to others, we attract friendly people. When we support others and celebrate their progress, we attract people who will do the same for us. We all need a squad behind that will encourage us and support us on our journey towards success.

If you're still reading this book, I know you want to be the best possible version of YOU. As you're growing, becoming more positive and more goal-oriented, know this: some of your peers will get jealous. They're going to think you're corny, and they're going to try to put you down. You MUST know who you are. Be confident in the fact that your life does not revolve around their opinion. And here's the thing: your life does not end during your school years. You have a great future ahead of you. This is just a season, and it's a time of preparation for what's to come.

And truth be told, there *may* be adults in your life who will envy your courage when you decide to take responsibility for your life and strive to be the best you can be. Minimize your time with them, and guard your mind and heart against negativity, jealousy, and unfair criticism.

When you select your squad, don't limit friendships and support from your peers only. There *are* parents, teachers, and other adults in your life that want the best for you and will help you along the way. I would strongly encourage you to ask a successful adult in your life, to mentor you. Having a mentor changed my life and it can change yours. Mentors have life experience that you can learn from that may keep you from making unnecessary mistakes. Be teachable and learn valuable lessons that can keep you from future regret and lead you to success.

Keep in mind that everyone, including you, has a unique story. We start at different places and with different experiences, resources, and support. Therefore, never compare your journey to someone else's. Your journey is yours. Embrace it. When we compare ourselves to others, we are telling God that He made a mistake when He created us. There is nothing about you that's a mistake.

Just like you are unique with your own story, so are other people. Every person you meet is just as valuable as you are. Unfortunately, many people don't know or believe this, so it shows up in the way they treat others. We can't control others, remember? But we can control ourselves.

I think when we peel off the layers, everybody wants the same thing. We want to be accepted for who we are. We want to accomplish things. We want to use our gifts and talents, and we want to know that we have a purpose and believe that we can achieve that purpose. These commonalities can serve as a bridge to connect us to each other.

The people in your squad don't have to be the same age, the same ethnicity, or have the exact same interests for you to learn from them. We all have strengths and weaknesses. We all have storms in our lives and things that will try to keep us from being successful. Having the right kind of support system through healthy relationships makes the journey of life more fun and fulfilling. It also makes us more resilient.

I cannot stress this enough: choose your squad wisely. Be the kind of person to others you want in your own life. Keep an open mind about people who are different from you. You may be very surprised with what you discover. Maybe you'll gain an unexpected friend as I did in Jenny. They should be positive, have good character and intentions, and have goals for themselves. My squad is very culturally diverse, and I have friends from all walks of life. However, I am careful about who I call a "friend." Being selective and intentional about my relationships has helped me become the person I am today. Either way, your squad will help you through tough times and offer the support you need to succeed in school, college, and life.

REFLECTION: Who is in your squad? Do they share the same goals as you? _____

_____

_____

_____

_____

_____

_____

_____

GO GETTER GOAL: Is there anyone in your "friends" circle that you know is not good for you? What makes them a potential threat to influencing/impacting you in a negative way? Decide to cut ties with those people on your list. Be cool with them, but don't hang out with them. (Use initials or code names, if needed to avoid the possibilty of gossip/arguments).

_____

_____

_____

_____

_____
_____
_____
_____

HIGH ACHIEVER CHALLENGE: Is there someone in your environment that you admire (their character, drive, and focus to be their best) but have been hesitant to connect with them because they are different from you? What are you afraid of? Are you willing to be open-minded towards others who are positive yet different from you? Do you have a mentor? If not, who do you know that you consider successful and would like to learn from? Take the first step and reach out to connect with them.

_____
_____
_____
_____
_____
_____
_____
_____

AFFIRMATION:

"I am surrounded by positive and driven friends and supporters!"

VI. Avoid Future Regret

"We must all suffer one of two things: the pain of discipline or the pain of regret or disappointment."
~ Jim Rohn

<u>From My Journal:</u> <u>*Drowning* (Age 14)</u>

It was summer time. I was selected for the Summer Youth Employment Program. I ended up being sent to a nursing home called West Lawrence Care Center (WLCC). WLCC was my first official "on the books" job. My boss was impressed with my work ethic and hired me after the summer program ended. I then worked part-time after school, each day to help support myself through high school.

I was so grateful because I desperately needed the money. I indulged myself in my work. I took pride in what I did. I developed close relationships with the seniors who were patients there and, over time, many of the co-workers. I loved being at work because it was my home away from home. I felt like I had found a family. More than anything, it was my safe haven. It kept me off the streets.

During the time I was in the summer program, I met Scotch and a few other teens who were working with us at WLCC. Scotch started out being just a co-worker, but we became friends pretty quickly. One day, we made plans to go to the beach after our workday was over. We simply had to cross the street on Seagirt Boulevard and we were there. It was a hot summer day, and the ocean looked beautiful—captivating. It was the only thing I loved about Rockaway.

We started going into the water one by one to cool down. Scotch and a few of the girls were playing around, splashing water at each other. As I walked into the water, it was refreshing. I jumped over the small waves and made my way into the ocean a little deeper. Another wave, another jump. I was in far enough to feel cooled down and felt the adrenaline rush as I saw another wave approaching. I jumped. I was safe. The water was still around my neck. I was standing confidently. I was awed by the natural beauty around me.

In a matter of minutes, I felt the sand beneath my toes disappear, and my head went under. I felt my insides filling up with water as I caught glimpses of water and blurred images of the people and things around me. I was in a panic as I felt myself fade out and gasp for even an ounce of air in my lungs. I could feel my insides filling with more water. In my mind, death was upon me.

Suddenly, I heard Scotch's voice as he grabbed my arm, trying to lift me above the water. I was in such panic that I pushed him under and was causing both of us to struggle with the fierceness of the ocean. It was nothing but a miracle from the angels above that I was grabbed and pulled out by a strong arm on both sides of my body. When I regained consciousness upon the sand, I saw the lifeguard whom, along with Scotch, saved my life.

The beaches of Rockaway had a reputation for beautiful but fierce waters. Every summer, people traveled from all over to experience the grains of sand, welcoming waters, and picturesque views. The waters were tricky though. You never knew what to expect with them. I had heard of countless stories through the years about people drowning in them. I never expected that I'd come so close to almost being one of those stories.

As I reflected on that moment, all I remember is that he was a slim athletic-built Spanish guy who wore bright neon swimwear. As he walked away, I wanted to say, "Thank you so much," but I was drained. I was terrified. I was in total shock. Scotch sat beside me, yelling at me in his loving kind of way, "You crazy! I was tryin' to help you, and you tryin' to kill me. Dang, glad you're ok now. You ok?"

After that day, Scotch and I became inseparable. Best friends. More like family. We were like brother and sister. Where you saw one, you saw the other.

Look Up and Beyond Strategy #6: Avoid Future Regret

I am thankful that I am here to talk about that day on the beach, but I am also thankful for the time I spent at WLCC because I gained valuable life lessons that help me make good decisions to this day, so many years later. I want to share the one I feel is MOST important so that you can learn it too. It has nothing to do with the beach, but it does have something to do with drowning.

I worked in the recreation department, and we were responsible for making sure that the seniors had fun and therapeutic things to do. We hosted birthday parties, themed events for special holidays, sports days, field trips, barbecues during the summer, and of course Bingo. I found out that seniors LOVE Bingo, and they take it VERY seriously. I almost witnessed two people, both in wheelchairs, ready to fight over Bingo!

My job was to visit the seniors' room, invite them to the activities, and transport them to the room where the activity was being held if needed. Some seniors would hang out in the dayroom where nursing staff would oversee them within a group. Most of the recreational activities happened in that room. After working there for a while, I noticed there were two groups of people living in the nursing home. Regardless of their ethnicity, religious background, socioeconomic status, political beliefs, and personal life experiences, they fit into one of two groups.

One group was a group of people that were content, positive, involved, and engaged. They were the friendliest people when you came to visit them and transport them from one place in the building to another. The seniors in this group had a peace about them that is really hard to explain in words. I've had the privilege to speak with and spend time with many of these seniors after work hours. I listened to their stories, their accomplishments, their failures, and lessons learned. I became very close to many of them and to this day still have their pictures and even poems they wrote to me. I didn't realize it at the time, but I gained wisdom beyond my years because of those interactions. I also gained temporary "grandparents," which helped me deal with the separation of my biological grandparents.

This first group of seniors wasn't necessarily happy about being in a nursing home; truth is, most were not. BUT these seniors made the best of it. They knew that they were at a place in their life where they didn't know how much time they had left, and they chose to have a good attitude. I would say this group of seniors lived their last days with purpose, which gave them a good quality of life. They spent those years giving life their best as they had done up to that point. And when they died, they died with peace and purpose. What a powerful thing!

Now, if you are still reading this and wondering what this has to do with you… I'll tell you. But, first, let's look at the other group of seniors.

The next group of seniors, well, they were the exact opposite of the first group. These seniors were discontent, miserable, complainers, and often very rude. No matter how you tried to encourage them, befriend them, and serve their need, they weren't happy. When I spoke with these seniors, they often reflected on their past. They complained about their mistakes and often blamed others for their misery. These seniors tried to isolate themselves in their rooms and refused many times to participate in anything recreational.

It was sad to witness. This group of seniors lived with immense regret. They were so focused on what life would've been if they did things differently back in the days. I still remember many of their faces; I remember the look of their pain of drowning in regret.

What tragedy it is to get to the end of your life, whatever age that may be, and live those last days in regret. Time is something that never goes back. And for all the choices we make, we must deal with the consequences, good or bad.

My friend, if you are reading this, I want to help you avoid future regret starting NOW. If you develop the habit of making good choices and doing your best, you will live a life of peace, happiness, and purpose. You will be successful in whatever you pursue on your academic and career journey.

So even in your youth, you can lay the foundation of a life rooted in good choices. This does not mean you will avoid mistakes or regrets completely. It simply means that you are walking in your power, making decisions consciously and taking responsibility to learn from every choice you made.

So, whether you are trying to decide whether or not to have sex with someone, try a drug for fun, steal something from someone you don't like just for personal revenge, or post something on social media just for attention, look at it carefully and ask yourself "In five to ten years from now when I am living the life I envision for myself, will my participation in this bring me **regret**?"

If you are not sure, **avoid it** altogether. Don't do it.

I know this is not always easy to do. BUT, it's possible. You have to remember your value, your vision, and your purpose. If you look deep enough, you WILL find the courage and strength to make the BEST decision, and you will avoid unnecessary pain.

Just on a side note, I would encourage you, in your youth to be open to listening to the seniors in your life. Spend time with your grandparents, if you are fortunate enough to know them, have them around, or can connect with them. If your grandparents are deceased, their legacy lives on through you. Think of all the lessons they taught you and apply them to your life. If you're open to this, I recommend you visit a nursing home and adopt a grandparent. Many of them are lonely. And if you're dealing with loneliness, you'd be surprised how much you may enjoy spending time with a senior.

Loneliness is a terrible thing. I have felt lonely for much of my life. Social media does not cure loneliness. You can have a million followers and still be drowning in loneliness. You can be a popular student and still feel lonely. And you can be more of a loner, like I was, and yearn for friendship and companionship so much that you engage in destructive behaviors. The best way to combat loneliness is to be a friend to others.

There is nothing unusual or corny about admitting your loneliness. It's an epidemic which means that countless people all over the world feel just like you do. We need human to human connection; it's how we were designed by God. If you study foundational psychology, you'll learn about a man named Abraham Maslow, known for "Maslow's Theory," which discusses human needs. Love and belonging are basic human needs. That's what human to human connection is supposed to foster.

If we don't get that connection in healthy ways, we become vulnerable to it in unhealthy and destructive ways. This sets us up to living a life of regret.

If we are aware and honest about our struggle with loneliness, we become empowered to do the things necessary to connect with others in healthy and meaningful ways.

Think about the choices you make each day and take the action that minimizes or erases the potential for regret. You will be so glad you did, especially in years to come. You don't have to drown in regret because you now have a life jacket of wisdom to make good decisions.

REFLECTION: What current regrets are you drowning in? What lessons have you learned from those regrets? Decide today, that you will forgive yourself for the part YOU played in the regret you feel.

_____

_____

_____

_____

_____

GO GETTER GOAL: Identify the things in your life that could possibly be setting you up for more/future regret.

List them all. _____

_____

_____

_____

_____

_____

_____

HIGH ACHIEVER CHALLENGE: Regarding the list you created, next to each situation, write down all the negative consequences you may face if you decide to do that thing. Will those consequences prevent you from reaching your academic, career, or life goals? Are you willing to pay the price of regret for something that may have no value to your potential and purpose?

_____

_____

_____

_____

_____

AFFIRMATION:
"I am making good choices daily!"

VII. Manage Life's Emotional Crisis & Distresses

"Pain is temporary. Quitting lasts forever."
~ Lance Armstrong

From My Journal: *Suicide (Age 15)*

"I want to die. My life doesn't matter. Everyone hates me."

Earlier that evening, Elmont kept going into my room as I sat on the bed trying to do my homework. He randomly kept showing up and cursing me out. I ignored him and kept studying. I had become accustomed to working under dysfunctional situations like this, so I pressed on. "I'm gonna be somebody," I thought and continued my work. He kept on. The fourth time, he grabbed the light bulb and twisted it out of the ceiling. Now I was in the dark. I was trying to remain calm. I felt the tears start to well up. I had a test the next day, and I wasn't in the mood for his drama.

He passed by the doorway every few minutes mumbling hateful things under his breath. Every word slapped my heart and stuck like glue. "Doesn't he get tired of this? Why does he hate me so much?" I pondered these things as I sat in the dark. After he took the light bulb out of my room, he locked himself in the bedroom with his beer.

Not long after, I heard arguing voices down the hall and they were rising. He started fighting with my mom, again. The kids were in the living room. Suddenly, things got physical. I got up and walked into the kitchen where they were at this point. Elmont was punching my mom. I started yelling, "Stop it! You're gonna hurt her!!" I jumped on him and started punching him on the head. He realized that I was hitting him and turned his attention to me. It was the first time I ever hit him back.

He hit me back but with hesitancy. Somehow, he was able to grab me by my neck. As he kept a strong tight grip on my neck, he lifted me and pushed me upward on the wall. I couldn't breathe. I felt my lungs hungry for air. He looked at me in my eyes, and I knew he wanted to kill me right there. My siblings jumped on him and shouted, "Stop it Daddy! You're hurting her! Stop it!"

He released me.

Elmont left the apartment for a few hours but came back acting as if nothing ever happened. I decided I would stay in my room. I had the light bulb back in, music playing in the background, and I was trying to study. It was late. I was tired. Elmont came back into my room and said, "Get out the room!"

I looked at him, cautiously responding, "Where am I supposed to sleep? What am I supposed to do?"

He looked at me, gave no response, and walked away.

Now, I was VERY tired. I was weary. I was angry. I wanted to die. I took three of the kitchen chairs and placed them beside each other to make a temporary bed. I tried to lie down, but I was restless in the midst of my exhaustion. I turned off the lights, lying down again only to get up a few minutes later. I was terrified of the roaches. I turned the light on, walked to the bathroom, and opened the medicine cabinet.

I saw bottles of pills prescribed to my mom. I didn't know what was for what. I didn't care. I wanted to take them all. I wanted to swallow them. I wanted out of this place. I grabbed two or three bottles, poured a glass of milk, and drank down one pill after the other. It seemed like forever, but after some gagging and crying, I was done. I lied down, wrapped my arms around myself, and cried myself to sleep. I hoped that the darkness in my eyes would soon bring some light of hope and peace.

I was awakened to the sound of my sisters and brother getting ready for school. It was the next day. My mom's voice was in the background telling them to move quickly. I sat up and collected my thoughts. They were all looking at me wondering why I was sleeping in the kitchen. I told them to mind their business. I got up and went into my bedroom. "I can't believe that I am still here," I thought in anger. A few minutes later, I took a shower, got dressed, and went to school.

Look Up and Beyond Strategy #7: Manage Life's Emotional Crisis & Distresses

After trying to take my own life not once but three times and living to talk about it, I can honestly say I have a passion and heart for bringing people hope. I just want you to hold on one more day, one more hour, one more minute, one more second if you are going through a TOUGH time right now.

Life does get better. It can change. But, after we take our last breath, that's it. It's OVER.

I don't believe God spent such intricate care creating you for you to die in pain and be defeated by it. When we destroy ourselves, we ultimately let pain win, but if we decide to manage our pain and find purpose in it, we WIN.

I am not only a three-time suicide attempt survivor, but I also take crisis calls speaking with people who want to end their life. One day, I received a call from a man who said he was on a bridge, ready to jump. He spoke angrily as he wept. I knew that in any moment, his life could possibly be over. Ultimately, it was HIS choice to die or live.

I began to pray and ask God for the right words to say to him. At first, he was not trying to listen to anything I said. I kept speaking words of hope. As I continued to speak, he began to calm down. Not only did he calm down, but he began to walk away from the bridge. Once he gained his composure and a sense of clarity, we spoke for a few hours. He confirmed what I already knew from personal experience and from listening to others in the same situation.

Here's the REAL deal about suicide: **People don't really want to die. They just want to escape the pain.**

When I was in my kitchen swallowing those pills, I honestly didn't want to die. I thought I did. I believed it very strongly in that moment, but feelings can create our mindset if we don't create our mindset to learn how to manage our feelings. It's all about learning how to cope with the negative emotions we feel from the negative experiences we experience.

Of course, I didn't know that as a young person. That's why I am here today to share the good news that it DOES get better.

When I woke up in that kitchen, no one knew what I had done. It had to be God that kept me from being physically sick. Afterwards, I thought about how traumatic it would have been for my young siblings to find my dead body in that kitchen. In my attempt to hurt Elmont, I would have only hurt those who sincerely loved me. That would not have been right.

And the truth is, Elmont didn't care about me if I was alive, so why would it hurt him if I died? I was giving him too much power over me. When I realized that, it changed everything for me. I began to heal in so many ways.

That man on the bridge sought professional counseling and learned the skills he needed to move forward and heal. You, too, can heal and move forward if you find yourself in a dark place emotionally. You don't have to get to that point where you're on a bridge or doing anything else dangerous with the intent of taking your own life.

Your perspective about your pain will make all the difference.

In a previous chapter, I spoke about focusing on what you CAN control versus what you can't. Remember, the two things you have control of in any situation are your attitude and your actions towards it. That takes discipline, but with the right mindset, you can develop the discipline you need to get through tough situations knowing you did the best you could.

I want to discuss ways for you to manage your emotions, especially in crisis or situations that cause distress. Whether you are being bullied in school, witnessing your parents' divorce, living in foster care, dealing with low self-esteem, or anything that creates negative and defeating emotions, you CAN learn to manage them.

If you don't learn how to manage your emotions, you will be at risk for self-sabotage, destruction, and ultimately failure. You must remember that you are unique and valuable, and you have a purpose that only YOU can live. Tough times never last, but tough people do. The practical strategies I share will strengthen you to overcome any difficulty you face in and outside of school.

Please note: these strategies and my advice does not replace medical advice. If you are dealing with mental illness, clinical diagnosis, and/or are under the supervision of a doctor, listen to them.

Look at these strategies and identify which ones you need to start applying in your life immediately. You deserve to live a life free of unnecessary emotional pain.

Forgive everyone that hurt you. This does not, in any way, justify their behavior towards you. Forgiveness is a decision that empowers you to move on with YOUR life. When you forgive, you release yourself from past trauma, hurt, and pain. **You may need to forgive yourself**. Guilt and regret can kill you slowly if not dealt with. People, all of us, will reap what we sow. Trust that without your revenge or any evil feelings towards them, they will have to reap for what they've done to you; it's a law that none of us can escape. Heal yourself and use your pain as a reason to treat others with respect and love. It will come back to you—guaranteed!

Take a piece of paper. Write down the name of EVERY person that you are mad at or have been hurt by even if they are not aware of it. Write down the offense, or what they did to you. If you are a spiritual person, pray for them. Then, release the person to the life that they must live. Take the paper and rip it up—or simply throw it out—and envision yourself now emotionally unattached from the people on the list. You are powerful for doing this!

As you know, I was bullied in elementary school. There was one particular girl. Let's call her Kathy. Well, Kathy was so mean. For years, she would instigate fights with me and others, or she simply would come up to me and start cursing me out to start a fight.

Well, after losing contact with her for years (I was happy about this—trust me), we reconnected on Facebook. I was hesitant to accept her friend request, but I did it anyway. I knew that I had forgiven her many years prior. We started to chat. Interestingly, when I brought up the fact that she used to torture me and how it affected me for many years, she told me that she didn't remember being that mean. After going back and forth, I realized that she sincerely forgot a lot of the bad things she did to me. She knew she was a bully, and she apologized, but she was very sincere in expressing that she didn't realize it was as bad as I was expressing it was.

If I had not forgiven her years before, I would've carried that emotional baggage with me. She had already gone on with her life, not giving ME a thought. If I had held onto what she did to me, it would've prevented me from being successful in life. And while her actions caused me trauma during our childhood years, I had the power to choose to not let her affect my life anymore. This in NO way says that what she did back then was okay. Because it was NOT. But me choosing to forgive her set ME FREE.

Our reconnection was a unique situation because we even met up some months later and stay connected on social media.

People do change over time. But they are not your problem. Make sure you don't get caught up in them. Some people will NEVER change. That's not your problem either. Focus on YOU and YOUR mental and emotional well-being.

I had to focus on myself and let go of all the bad things Elmont did to me for over fifteen years. He was supposed to be my protector, but he hurt me deeply. It wasn't just the physical hits that hurt but more so the vicious words he spoke. They were glued to the walls of my heart for a long time, and so much of my identity was wrapped up in the lies he spoke about me, to me.

I used to wish death upon Elmont and even daydreamed about killing him myself. I am glad that I never went through with those thoughts because I would be dead or in prison. I would've missed out on a great life because I allowed my destructive thoughts to take over.

You already know that I grew up in an abusive and dysfunctional home, but did I tell you that I was threatened to NEVER talk about our personal home life outside of home? My step-father actually threatened to kill me if I did. You may remember in Chapter 3 that I told someone in elementary school about the beatings I used to get at home. Well, a social worker did come to my home, but my step-father locked me in a room while he sat down in the living room with her, bad-mouthing me. He was known for his charming and quiet demeanor outside of the house. People thought he was the nicest guy. But it was just a show, and this woman was getting his best show.

I used to sit and wonder what made him the mean, manipulative, controlling, and just outright abusive man that he was. As I wondered, I felt sadness. I know that hurt people hurt people. And the more pain someone harbors in them, the more destructive they are to themselves and others.

When I started to think deep like that, I realized that I was NEVER the problem. It was ALWAYS him. He was just projecting his problems onto me because I was closest to him and vulnerable. Realizing this helped me to not only forgive him but see myself as the valuable person that I am and always was.

If I had killed him or done something else destructive and evil, it would have only made him look like the honest person he falsely portrayed himself to be. I would have proved him right, giving him too much power. Proving him wrong about me was one of my greatest motivations, to do something positive with my life for a long time.

That's how I became stronger mentally and emotionally.

After that realization, I made a vow to God, myself, and my family that I would NEVER again even entertain the thought of hurting and/or killing myself.

We all think bad things sometimes. All of us. That doesn't make us bad people. What makes us bad is when we allow those bad thoughts to fester and shape us into a person we thought we'd never be. That's why it's important to monitor our thoughts. We can replace bad thoughts with good ones. It does take time, energy, effort, and support, but it's so worth it.

If deep emotional damage is done, it can take years to undo, but the great thing is this: time passes anyway, so we have something great to look forward to in the future knowing that we are on our growth and healing journey.

Here are some of the strategies I used to cope with negative thoughts and emotions:

Change the things you watch, read, and listen to when you notice they cause you emotional distress. If you've never paid attention to this, I challenge you to do it from this day forward. Take control of your life by managing your emotions. Identify the things that trigger negative emotions. It could be TV shows, movies, music, conversations with others, and/or things you read. Start to eliminate the negative things as much as possible. Instead, choose uplifting, enlightening, and empowering things that make you feel positive and good. What you allow to take into your consciousness affects you more than you realize.

I used to suffer from depression—especially seasonal depression. Every October until about March, I felt this dark cloud over me. I cried a lot. I was always tired. I had so many negative thoughts running through my mind. I hated positive and happy people. I was just miserable.

When I started my personal development journey, I read books that revealed that I had more power over my depression that I thought. I began to do the same things I encourage you to do in this chapter.

One of the main things I figured out was affecting me was

the television. I am a visual person and watching the news and certain other shows left me emotionally drained. They were the triggers to depression, so I stopped watching TV. I'm not telling you to do that unless you want to, but what I am going to tell you is this: over time, my mood changed. It took some time, and I had to keep "starting over" until managing my emotions became a habit. I have not been depressed in years. Today, I am a very positive person, and it has positively impacted my life personally and professionally. And, I also do watch some TV.

Take time to self-care. This means that you become a student that is aware of who you are, why you're that way, and how you can improve yourself. You commit to learning, but you also make time to rest, eat well, and assess your beliefs, values, and spirituality. Just because you're young, don't assume that you can live life without consequences. To be in control of your life, you must be aware and intentional about caring for yourself as a whole person. You have a physical, emotional, mental, and spiritual part of you. All of these parts make you whole. Therefore, you should be aware of all parts and make good decisions that positively affect your entire being. This empowers you to be resilient during even the toughest times you may face.

Reaching Out Beyond the Pain

Before I end this chapter, I want to talk about the power of reaching out for help. I grew up in a culture that shamed it. Remember, even though I am White, my family and the community I grew up in and live in is predominantly Black. Growing up, all throughout my childhood, teen years, and young adult years, I kept hearing the same story about how important it is to keep your personal and family business at home. I was taught that it's weak to ask for help. My step-father and many others used to say, "Only weak people go to counseling."

I spent four years of my youth harboring bad emotions and refusing to cry in an attempt to show others that I was strong. I used to believe that I had to carry these things to my grave because opening up to others meant I failed them and myself. Those were four long years where I almost destroyed myself.

Although this mindset is prevalent in the Black community, it does cross other cultural borders. And the truth is, regardless of our race, cultural background, or even religious beliefs, we all share the **human experience**. We all have troubles and trials that we must overcome. If cultural stigmas are keeping us in a prison of negative and destructive thoughts, we must break free from that. We can respect our culture and family heritage even though we choose to reach out beyond that, to get help. This is REAL strength.

The irony in all of this is that the same people who told me "keep your business at home" and "seeing a counselor is weak" are the same people who were struggling with mental health issues the most. They needed the help. Patterns of dysfunction were passed down from one generation to the next, simply because people refused to seek professional help.

I did not want to be part of that continuous cycle; I knew at a young age that I did not want to be like those people. I loved many of them. And in no way did I—or do I—think I'm better than them. I just knew that something was wrong with their philosophy about life and their lifestyle. I was determined to not repeat it. I was inspired to grow and become better.

As I grew stronger emotionally and mentally, I was able to be an encourager to many of the same people from my childhood, teen and young adult years. Yes, I was able to empower them and speak words of hope into their life because I made the decision to follow a different path. A healthy path. A path where I reached out for help and knew that this was REAL strength.

Here's the deal:

We ALL need help at some point.

Life is too difficult, complex, unfair, and burdensome at times to carry the emotions of these experiences within without healthy release and support. Trying to do that is setting ourselves up for failure.

So, wherever you find yourself, keep in mind that you are valuable and have a purpose.

No matter how difficult of a time you're going through, PLEASE hold on and also reach out.

REFLECTION: Do you forgive people easily and keep it moving? Or do you hold grudges and anger inside of you because of the actions of others? Are you stuck because of unforgiveness? Explain.

_____

_____

_____

_____

_____

_____

_____

_____

GO GETTER GOAL: Follow through on the exercise I shared in this chapter on forgiveness. Create your list. Identify the pain. Make peace with it, discard the list, and envision your freedom from emotional prison. Take this space to write about how you feel afterwards.

_____

_____

_____

_____

_____

_____

_____

_____

_____

HIGH ACHIEVER CHALLENGE: Identify what your triggers are (social media/TV/music/negative friends) and create a plan to eliminate those things. What will you replace them with?

_____
_____
_____
_____
_____
_____
_____

Because of the heaviness of this chapter, I wanted to create an extra space for discussion, reflection, and healing. **_Beyond the Pain_** is designed to help you dig deeper and identify the root causes of your emotional pain, distress, and possibly suicidal thoughts. It is also for you to create a plan for support. I need the support of others to be my best. You need the support of others to be your best. WE ALL NEED someone. There is NOTHING weak or shameful about that. I promise you.

Beyond the Pain: **Do you struggle with suicidal thoughts?**

_____
_____
_____

What do you think triggers these thoughts?

_____
_____
_____
_____
_____

Have you reached out for help and support? If not, why not? Identify a trustworthy adult that you can go to. *(Make sure this adult is emotionally and mentally healthy.)*

_____

_____

_____

_____

_____

Get Connected:
National Suicide Prevention Hotline: 1-800-273-8255

AFFIRMATION:
"I am managing my emotions!"

VIII. Set Goals and Take Action

**"You are not what happened to you." ~
Jessica Janniere**

From My Journal: *Jail Time (Age 16)*

"Jessss, you ok?" I heard my mom's dragging voice from across
the lockup cells. She was in her cell with about six or seven other
women who were there for God knows what. She was scared.
And she was scared for me. She was drained, and she felt like
giving up. I heard it in her voice. "I'm ok, Ma...I'm good." I yelled
out loud enough to give her some assurance as I sat in my cell.

I was in my cell with a Spanish girl who was sitting on a
hard-wooden bench, crying. As I looked around, I was disgusted
with the cold walls, the silver metal toilet with no seat, the dirty
white sink in the corner, and the metal bars that hid me from
the cruel world outside. "So, this is what jail is like," I thought.
I didn't like it at all. From the transport ride to the check-in
process, I felt like an animal. My wrists hurt from the handcuffs
that squeezed my skinny wrist bones.

When I arrived at the check-in point, I was searched,
touched, and spoken to harshly. Going through the process, I
better understood how many of my street friends ended up in
a cycle of coming in and out of this system; there's something
very psychologically damaging about it. I was stuck in a system
that didn't care about my story. They didn't know me. I was a
perpetrator, a criminal to them, and I was treated like everyone
else even though I was a victim.

The loud sounds of the banging cell gates must have stirred
my mom, and once again she yelled out, "Jess, you're back?"

"Yes, Ma, I'm back. I'm good."

"Ok honey, I love you," she whined, and it was starting to irritate me.

"I love you, too, Ma." I said it just quick enough for her not to hear my irritation with her. She was going through enough; I didn't want to add to her pain. The lights were turned down, and a few officers seemed to be making rounds. Every now and then, you'd hear someone arguing, someone getting cursed out, or just metal cell gates clinging and clanging as they opened and closed.

The hours dragged on, and after a while, you'd lose sense of what time and day it was. Your mind would wander, and emotions would stir based on your thoughts. It was a vulnerable feeling for me as I tried to think ahead about my future. It just looked so bleak, so gray—no, it looked real dark. I understood why some people snap and go crazy.

Many of them are simply misunderstood, their voices never heard in the midst of a system that is covered in constant noise. It's like being drowned out in a loud room. You're crying out for help, but no one hears you. They see your body language and your frustration, but it's misinterpreted. They don't know your heart. They only see you based on their own perception of you, and that's scary because all of us have a limited perspective. Many of us have a twisted perspective because of our own wounds and baggage.

I felt angry and wanted to scream, but instead, I believed strength was in remaining quiet and looking strong. In my world, I had been conditioned to smile when, on the inside, I was weeping. I would strive to cover up my pain and show the world they can't have the satisfaction of seeing me down. I was very motivated to survive and thrive, but I was carrying too much. I was finding unhealthy outlets for my pain, and my moments of strength were built on superficial things; that's why I kept falling on my face.

Look Up and Beyond Strategy #8: Set Goals and Take Action

The greatest battle we will ever fight is the one in our mind. Our thoughts can literally put us in a prison that limits us from becoming the successful person we desire to be. As we prepare to identify your goals, continue to focus on replacing negative thoughts with positive ones. I also want to help you define what success means to YOU.

In our culture, society somehow shapes our mind to believe that we are ONLY successful if we look a certain way, have a certain number of social media followers, college degrees, high profile titles, and, of course, lots of money. These things do have their place and value, but those things should not define us, and not everyone is interested in pursuing them. That's okay.

Here's what I want to propose to you. How do YOU define success? Think about this deeply and be honest with yourself. Don't worry about what people might say if they knew your answer. You don't live your life for other people. It's YOUR life. The answer to this should tie into your vision and purpose. Even if you don't see the connection now, don't worry. Just stay true to who you are and who you're becoming. It'll all make sense at the right time.

Imagine that you have no limitations. Think about a life where you have all the time, money, friends/connections, credentials, education, and experience you need to accomplish any goal you set for yourself. Imagine yourself being a person who was confident, clear on your purpose, energetic, happy, and fearless. Hold that image of yourself in your mind. If your life was "perfect" like you just imagined, what goals would you set for yourself?

Make a list of every goal you would pursue. Don't worry about your current circumstances. This is your time to look up and beyond to the future you imagine. Once you have your list, take the top three things listed. Those are most likely your immediate short-term goals. We are going to break them down with specific tasks that you can do to get you closer to achieving your goals.

In my experience with goal setting, I realized the following: Your goals are for you. Drown out the outside voices—especially those telling you who to be if it's not true to who you really are.

Goals change as we change. Don't get so attached to a goal that you miss the lesson of progress along the way.

You won't hit every goal. Don't beat yourself up about it. Most successful people will tell you that they fail more than they succeed when pursuing their goals. I'm sure that sounds strange, but it's true. We'll talk more about that later.

The basics of effective goal setting will help you identify what you want and how to get it for every area of your life.

Even when you're going through tough times, you can still pursue your goals. You may need to make some adjustments, but the important thing is to never quit.

Since you are a student, let's talk about some practical ways you can achieve your academic goals.

- Decide what you want. Be specific and write down WHY you want to achieve this goal.

- Set a deadline. By when do you want to accomplish this goal?

- Identify the obstacles you need to overcome to achieve this goal.

- List any skills you need to achieve this goal.

- Write down a list of people who can help/support you in achieving your goal.

- Make a list of everything you need to do to achieve your goal.

Now, create a practical plan.

Here's a sample of this goal setting strategy using the outline above:

- I want to graduate with honors.

- I want to graduate on time.

- My obstacles are laziness, poor study habits, parents' divorce and fighting, and financial stress because Mom is now alone.

- The skill I need to achieve my goal is developing better study habits.

- The people that can support me are my guidance counselor and my best friend.

- In order for me to accomplish my goal, I need self-discipline, a structured study time, an outlet for my hurt over the divorce, and a part-time job to help with the financial stress at home.

Here's my plan:

My mom is my WHY. I don't want her to hurt anymore, so I am going to make her proud. I will carry her picture with me as a reminder when I feel discouraged or lazy.

I will identify where my grades are and how I can improve them. Then, I will speak to the top student in my class and see if they're open to studying with me. Also, I will try look for an accountability partner. If they are not open to this, I will ask my guidance counselor for suggestions or inquire about after school tutoring.

I don't have control over my parents' divorce. I can only control my attitude and my actions. Although I am very hurt by all of this, I will use my energy in a positive way to achieve my goals. I will make sure I maintain a positive attitude through it all. This will also help my Mom and others affected by the divorce.

I will see if there are any part-time jobs I can apply to. I need to create a resume. Then, apply to jobs. I can also consider starting a small business to generate some income. For ideas on what to do and how to do it, type something like **Business Ideas for Teens** in your Google search.

Now that you have this plan, you know exactly what to do.

Here's the bottom line: if you're setting goals and pursuing them with a good attitude and strategy, you are already ahead of countless students. You are already positioned to make it far in life. Tough times, failure, and even fear will not be able to stop you. They will challenge you, but if you keep moving forward with the right attitude and action, you will become more resilient and will see amazing progress.

REFLECTION: When it comes to setting and pursuing your goals, what's your biggest challenge and/or obstacle? Explain.

_____

_____

_____

_____

_____

_____

GO GETTER GOAL: Follow through on the exercise I shared in this chapter on goal setting. Write out your plan for at least 3 of your immediate goals.

_____

_____

_____

_____

_____

_____

_____

HIGH ACHIEVER CHALLENGE: Share your plan with someone you trust. Ask them to hold you accountable and check in with you about your progress. Who is this person and why do you trust them?

_____

_____

_____

_____

_____

AFFIRMATION:

"I am a goal getter!"

IX. Face Your Fears

"I learned that courage was not the absence of fear, but the triumph over it. The brave man is not he who does not feel afraid, but he who conquers that fear." ~ **Nelson Mandela**

From My Journal: *Planning My Escape (17)*

I sat in the passenger side of the recruiter's car. He was making small talk with me as he drove, asking me about my goals and dreams. I was impressed with the fact that he traveled from Brooklyn all the way to Far Rockaway to pick me up. His polished uniform and stoic expression was very intimidating. I kept it very generic as I replied, "Well, I feel like I need to just get away from here, discover my gifts and talents, and do something productive with my life." He nodded his head and listened attentively.

As we arrived at Fort Hamilton Army Base, I felt anxiety consume me. I could feel my neck and chest getting hot. I always broke out in hives when I had inner turmoil, and it was happening again despite me trying to be cool. I went through the physical exam and testing process not too long after we arrived in the large building. I had to give urine to a female officer watching me pee. That was weird. "I guess this will all be worth it," I thought as I followed the instructions given.

I wanted to get away from home as I reminisced about all the drama that surrounded my life. I asked my mother to sign papers that would allow me to join the Army Reserves. She did. Things were crazy. Legal battles were still dragging on. Vicky was becoming more distant and rebellious. I was getting bored at WLCC; I wanted to explore the world. It was justified. Made sense to me. It didn't take long for me to get a call from the Recruiter saying I had been accepted. I had signed the agreement that I would serve six years. A minimum of four years would be full-time active duty service after Basic Training. I was excited.

In preparation for this move, I showed up at 766 Quartermaster one weekend a month. Although I was in plain clothing, I had to participate just like the other soldiers. I was very uncomfortable and kept to myself. My best memory from that year was learning how to assemble and disassemble an M60 machine gun. I was scheduled to leave for Basic Training a few months after my graduation that June. I never made it there because I never graduated. I dropped out.

I seemed to hit a point where I couldn't function properly. I was very emotional and cried at the drop of a dime. I felt this deep darkness around my mind. I was smoking and drinking all night and sleeping all day. I had absolutely no interest in school and could not concentrate on anything. I tried to cover up my pain with jokes, but within me, there was a war raging. It was the battle of desiring more and wanting to quit. Life just seemed so confusing. I barely made it to work and lived in a distant bubble for a long time.

I humbled myself and made an appointment to see a therapist. I needed an outlet. My therapist was a skinny and petite older Jewish woman who tried not to look shocked when I confided to her about some of my traumatic experiences. But, she was very friendly. I realized years later that I simply needed a healthy outlet to express my emotions and experiences. It was the beginning of my healing journey. Six months later, I picked myself up and went back to finish high school to complete the few credits I needed. I graduated with honors and felt good about my decision. By this time, I was dishonorably discharged from the Army.

Look Up And Beyond Strategy #9: Facing Those Fears

After getting discharged from the Army, I felt lost. I didn't know what my next move would be. I knew that I needed to escape my negative environment. I felt like a failure. All of my hopes and dreams seemed tied to that opportunity.

It took me some time to learn that I was simply being redirected to a different path. In no way was I a failure. Failure was one of my biggest fears, but the truth is I had **many** fears that kept me from making the progress I wanted to make.

Let's look at some of the most common fears that keep students from discovering their full potential. Many of them are connected to each other.

Fear of people:
Fear of people comes from our need to be validated by people. This gives others too much power over you. When we fear people, we fear their reaction to our decisions. Therefore, we make decisions based on them, never our true selves. If you fear people and don't deal with that issue, you will be very miserable. Don't do that to yourself. Be true to yourself by remembering your value and purpose. It comes from God, not people. Therefore, fear God, not people.

Fear of failure:
No one wants to lose at anything, but in order to grow, we must be willing to fail in our attempts sometimes. If we fear mistakes, setbacks, and disappointments, we will miss the opportunity to grow and experience success. Every successful person has a storybook of failures and the mindset that failure is a stepping stone to success. There's no way around it. Failure is an event, not a person.

Fear of success:
This may sound ironic, but many people are afraid of success.

We fear what other people may think if we let our light shine. We wonder if we can handle the success. We also question if we deserve to succeed. I am here to tell you—in case you need to hear it—you deserve to have success, whatever that looks like to you. Don't fear it. Prepare for it, work for it, expect it, and value it.

Fear of rejection:

This fear is deeply connected to fear of people. We want to be accepted by others, and sometimes we will face rejection. Rejection is nothing more than a redirection. When you're rejected, understand that you're rejected from experiences but never as the valuable person you are. Rejection can move you from where you thought you were supposed to be to where you *really* need to be.

Fear of change/ unknown:

It is human nature to want to be in control of things, but there are times in our lives when we must understand that we can't control people, situations, or outcomes. During those times, we must have faith. When change is upon us and we don't know what to expect, fear can try to take over. Fear of change tends to worry and create all these different scenarios in our head that feed our fears. When that happens, have faith. The things you're worried about most likely won't happen. Faith will carry you through and give you an optimistic attitude that things will work out.

With so many fears, it's no wonder many students don't live up to their full potential or discover their purpose. Fear is debilitating. It is consuming. But it doesn't have to be.

I want to empower you to have the right mindset about these fears so you are not hindered by them. Fear is nothing more than **f**alse **e**vidence **a**ppearing **r**eal. It's an emotion that causes an illusion. There is no way to get rid of fear completely, but you can minimize the effects of it in your life. You can succeed at achieving your goals, untapping your potential, and ultimately walk in your purpose.

There are two ways to manage fear:

Change your perspective about it.

Take action despite feeling afraid.

Let's look at why you might fear failure. Failure is one of those things that no one likes to experience. Whether losing the game on a sports team, failing a test, or making a mistake, failure doesn't feel good. Aside from that, we tend to allow failures to define us.

If you fail a class, it doesn't mean that you're a failure. It means that there's a reason you failed the test. Was it testing anxiety? Did you get lazy and not study? Are you going to take responsibility and recognize what part you played in failing the class?

Embrace failure. Failure is your friend. When you pursue your goals and fail to meet them, failure gives you an indication that something needs to be changed. This is a good thing. Redefine how you see failure. Look at it as an opportunity, not an obstacle.

Keep in mind that no matter what you do, it's impossible to remove fear entirely. Fear can be a good thing. It's a protective method used to keep you from danger. It can cause you to hesitate and think before you act, but when you know you are safe and ready to take action, you must feel the fear and move anyway.

If you're thinking about applying to a post-secondary school or internship out of the state, you most likely will encounter fear. It may creep up and try to talk you out of it. Your initial reaction might be that you are comfortable remaining where you are because you are familiar with everyone and everything. Once you know that you've done your research, and everything is credible, activate your faith and courage and move forward. Apply. You never know.

Don't let fear stop you from taking risks that can improve your life. There is so much to explore in life. Allow school and your current experiences to help you prepare for those opportunities. Make a commitment to yourself to not allow fear to stop you from living life fully. Refuse to be put in a box. If you feel like you're in one now, refuse to stay there.

You only have one life. Live it courageously, and you'll leave your powerful print in this world one day.

REFLECTION: What are you afraid of? Why?

_____

_____

_____

_____

_____

GO GETTER GOAL: Take the fears you listed and research the root cause. Look at them. Make peace with them, and commit to walking in faith and courage, not fear. Describe this process for you. How do you feel? What did you learn about yourself?

_____

_____

_____

_____

_____

HIGH ACHIEVER CHALLENGE: What is one risk you can take that will improve your life? How will it improve your life?

_____

_____

_____

_____

AFFIRMATION:

"I am courageous!"

X. Turn Pain Into Purpose

"He who has a why to live can bear almost any how."
~ Friedrich Nietzsche

From My Journal: *When Tragedy Hits (Age 18)*

I woke up to a living nightmare. Vicky's life took a drastic turn. I was at WLCC and received a call from my mom who was on the other line weeping, hysterical. Difficult to understand her, I was pushed to move quickly just from the emotion in her voice. I told my boss Ellen what was happening. We rushed out and jumped in her car.

Upon arriving, I ran upstairs and entered the kitchen. I saw my mother crying, overwhelmed with fear and anxiety. She began to explain hysterically that she received a visit from a detective. He had brought pictures of an unidentified teen girl who was brought to the hospital unconscious and severely burned. She wept and screamed. I told her, "OK, let's be calm about this. We'll go to the precinct, and I'll look at the pictures."

Once we arrived at the 100th precinct, we asked for the detectives. They took us to an interrogation room. They took Shelly and Dre (my girlfriend and Vicky's boyfriend at the time) out and spoke to them on the side in another room. The detectives asked us a few questions and then showed me the photo of the girl known as Jane Doe. The quality of the photo was not very good. The girl's face was slanted, so you couldn't see the entire front profile. Then, her face was extremely big like a balloon; swollen. A tube was coming out of her nose. It was hard to tell.

"Is there a way I could go see the unidentified girl in person? I would know if it's my sister if I saw her." They agreed and offered to drive us into Manhattan to Cornell Medical Center.

They had a special burn unit where the young girl was admitted. She was severely burned after being found in an abandoned building that was set on fire.

During the drive there, I chatted with the detectives. They wouldn't give too much info about the case. One of them, Detective McCaffer, was really nice and tried to answer my questions as best as possible. We finally reached the hospital. It was so large. The sick feeling intensified as we took the elevator up. As we exited the elevator, we were introduced to a nurse who gave us a brief overview of the girl's condition. She really did try to prepare us, but when we walked into that room and pushed back the curtain, I felt numb.

The nurse then removed the hair cap from the unidentified girl. My heart felt numb. I knew deep down inside of me that it was Vicky. I asked the nurse to show me her ankle. When I saw it, I recognized the burn marks that I cleaned just a few days prior. They were gang initiation marks.

Standing there, I found the strength to muster the words, "Oh my God, this is Vicky. This is Vicky." I could hear my mother go hysterical; it was the deep weeping from the soul and heart of a mother, a pain that goes beyond words. There were no words for this, and I began to cry. I think I went into shock. The reality of this was so hard to accept.

I stood there in that hospital room, and so many memories flashed back through my mind. I held on to that last day, that day when I was gentle. I was loving, and I spoke words of kindness to her. I cleaned her wounds. I showed her the best way I knew possible that she was special, not knowing that would be our last moment together. I hold on to that day many years later, and I recognize that a higher power intervened and helped me. I am so grateful. Everything after that seemed to go so fast, yet it seemed like life was at a standstill.

During the few days we went back and forth to the hospital, I found myself praying that God would take Vicky to Heaven. I believed that earth was Hell, so any place away from here had to be better. And maybe, just maybe Heaven existed, especially for people like my sister, young people who had their lives taken so suddenly. I wanted her to rest. She had been through enough. If she was brain damaged, she would have no quality of life.

A few days later, the test results came back, and it was found that Vicky was brain dead. They were taking her off life support the next day, on Thanksgiving Day.

Look Up and Beyond Strategy #10: Turn Pain into Purpose

Life.

It's so unpredictable at times.

Yet, at the same time, it is predictable.

What makes it predictable is that we all kind of know that life comes with pain, adversity, and living through tough times. However, I don't think most of us are taught that this is inevitable, so we are not prepared for it. On top of that, we are expected to just figure it out how to deal with it along the way. As a young person, this can be very overwhelming while navigating school, sports/extracurricular activities, and a social life.

When my sister was murdered, it changed everything. Initially, I was the one who had to be strong for my family, especially my mom. There was this constant pressure to be the "adult" and always appear to be okay. After we buried Vicky, I realized that I needed time to grieve. Depression overtook me for some time until I sought help. I knew that I didn't want to be dependent on a system. I knew that despite being victimized much of my life, no one owed me anything. I had to take personal responsibility for my life. It was so painful.

I had to make a decision, and I had to make it quickly. I had to decide that I would no longer allow my pain to be identity and I would use it for a greater purpose.

I don't know what you're going through in your life, but I want to tell you from the bottom of my heart that you can make it through, and you can turn your pain into purpose. That means that within the painful circumstances of your life are opportunities to do something positive and good.

There are countless examples we can look to for inspiration on how to do this.

Let's look at Nick Vujicic, a man who was born without limbs. His family thought he would be a basket case for all the days of his life. Nick was bullied in school and had a hard time understanding why God allowed him to be born this way. He struggled a lot throughout his life with self-acceptance and wondered what his purpose was. Today, Nick is a family man, married with children, a best-selling author, and a successful entrepreneur and motivational speaker. He does everything "normal" people do despite his disability. He took responsibility for his life. And he used his pain and turned it into purpose.

Have you ever heard of Malala Yousafzai? She was only fifteen years old when she was shot in the face by a Taliban gunman. The Taliban wanted to kill her because they are against the advancement of girls and women, and Malala believes that it is a girl's fundamental right to be educated. Her advocacy and passion to empower girls with education, especially in a hostile and opposing environment, made her a target. She could've died, but she lived and turned her pain into purpose.

Les Brown was born with his twin brother in an abandoned building in a poor neighborhood. He was given up for adoption and adopted by a woman named "Mamie Brown." Les had learning disabilities and was labeled "mentally retarded" in elementary school. He suffered from low self-esteem and low confidence because of it. Statistically, Les should've been unsuccessful, but today he is one of the top motivational speakers in the world. He's had great career success in the fields of entertainment and politics as well. His inspirational messages impact countless people from all walks of life. Les took his pain and turned it into purpose.

I think of Helen Keller, Oprah Winfrey, and countless others who, despite their negative past and obstacles, went on to achieve great things while positively impacting the world. They found their WHY and figured out HOW along the way. They took their pain and turned it into purpose.

Stories like theirs have helped me to look up and beyond my own pain and at my purpose.

Vicky's death inspired me to become a better person with the hope of positively impacting young people from all over the world. I am naturally a shy and introverted person, but my newfound inspiration has me doing things I used to be afraid of. Purpose strengthens us to overcome our fears.

When we discover our WHY, we figure out the HOW. The acronym I use for the word why is **W**hat **H**urts **Y**ou. I knew that I did not want my sister's death to be in vain. It hurts me to know that because of her environment, poor choices, and painful past she ended up in a situation she could not get out of. She felt defined by those things. It hurts me to know, every day, young people all around the world are going through the same thing. But, what hurts me is also what helps me.

What helps me is knowing that I have a story in me that could possibly save one young lady or man from a similar road, a road to destruction.

My WHY turned into my purpose, and my purpose helps me overcome my fears. The same thing will happen for you.

REFLECTION: What is your WHY? What hurts you?

_____

_____

_____

_____

_____

_____

_____

_____

GO GETTER GOAL: How can you take the thing that hurts you and use it as a stepping stone to discover your potential and purpose?

_____

_____

_____

_____

_____

_____

_____

_____

_____

HIGH ACHIEVER CHALLENGE: Research the lives of the people I mentioned in this chapter. Which one do you identify with? How can you use their life as an example to turn your pain into purpose?

_____

_____

_____

_____

_____

_____

_____

_____

AFFIRMATION:
"I am purpose driven!"

XI. Be Grateful

"Gratitude unlocks the fullness of life. It turns what we have into enough, and more. It turns denial into acceptance, chaos to order, confusion to clarity. It can turn a meal into a feast, a house into a home, a stranger into a friend." ~ Melody Beattie

From My Journal: *The Kind Deed* (Age 18)

It was Thanksgiving Day 1998. I was trying to count my blessings. I was really trying to be grateful for the good things in my life, but that day, it was hard. It seemed like life would never get better. We received the call from the hospital stating that Vicky was officially pronounced dead. My mother went into the room, fell out on her bed, and wept into her pillow. I sat silently in the living room. It was just the two of us now. I didn't really know how to console her, so I just left her alone.

The doorbell rang some time later, and I walked into my mom's bedroom, which was located at the front of the building. I looked out of the third-floor window, and it was Lucy, my co-worker from WLCC, standing outside of the building with her grocery cart. I yelled down to her, "Hey Lucy, do you need something?"

She looked up and replied, "Jess, come open the door. I have something for you and your mom. I just need a hand."

I grabbed my flip-flops, threw on a jacket, and walked down the stairs to meet Lucy. When I opened the door, she smiled slightly. "I made some food for you and your mom. I know today is not a good day, but you still have to eat at some point." I didn't think much about what she said. I simply thanked her as we both grabbed an end of the cart and made our way slowly up the stairs.

Once I got into the kitchen, she began to unpack her grocery cart, placing the items on the table and explaining each one. "This right here is some homemade mashed potatoes. Here is a green bean casserole. There's some cake too. And, Jess, I know you love stuffed mushrooms, so I made some just for you." She spoke softly and lovingly as she reached into the bottom of a plastic bag. When her hands came out, they held a foil tray pan that had a full turkey in it.

Lucy continued, "The turkey was freshly baked this morning. It has stuffing in it. I know you and your mom probably won't be hungry, I don't know, but I know at some point you'll have to eat. I wanted to do this for you. I'm so sorry about everything that's happened. I don't know what else to say or do. I feel so terrible. So sad. I'm gonna go home now." Her voice tapered off into silence.

I looked at the table filled with containers and pans of home-cooked food. It was a feast. I know Lucy had put her heart into preparing it for us. I also knew that when my mom woke up, she would need to eat something. She hadn't looked at food in days.

All I could say was, "Wow. Thank you, Lucy, you've done enough. This means a lot. Thank you for this kind deed, and happy Thanksgiving." I was so grateful, I cried.

Look Up and Beyond Strategy #11: Be Grateful

Gratitude is one of your greatest weapons to overcome the storms of life. No matter how difficult a situation is, it could always be worse. No matter what you're going through in school, at work, or at home, there is always something to be thankful for.

In this chapter, I want to equip you with the power of gratitude. Earlier, we talked about the benefits of having a positive attitude. Attitude does determine our altitude in life. Attitude will detract or attract success. Well, the foundation to a positive attitude is gratitude.

When we're going through tough times, it can be difficult to see the blessings we have, and the more we focus on our problems and what we don't have, the worse we feel and the weaker we become emotionally. We can train our mind to shift from what we don't have to what we do have.

Have you ever looked at a peer in your school or somewhere you were and envied them because they looked like they had the "perfect" life? Do you get jealous when you see other students and peers having success academically, socially, and career-wise? Jealousy will block your growth and blessings.

I used to be jealous of people all the time. I felt that everyone had it easier than I did and would "hate" on them without knowing them. I was just making assumptions based on what I saw. Well, here's what I learned as I grew up and started to mature: not everything that glitters is gold. Sometimes, looks can be deceiving.

It can seem like others have it easier than you, but it's not your job to focus on that. It's your job to take responsibility for you. When you do that, you can begin to look at all the great things you do have or the things that you have the ability to acquire.

We each have our own journey. And the truth is, you are unique. Your fingerprint should always remind you of this. That means that your life, circumstances, and experiences will be unique to you. Count your blessings and look at all the things you can be grateful for.

I'm telling you, when you have an attitude of gratitude, you become RESILIENT, STRONG, and UNSTOPPABLE.

Life does not have to be going the way you think it should go for you to be grateful. You choose to be grateful. It's something you CAN control.

There are so many benefits to being grateful. You will feel happier. You will be healthier. An ungrateful person complains a lot and is very envious of others. These emotions affect your health and state of mind. They can bring on sickness and lead to depression and other negative things.

Start to look around and within and identify what your

blessings are. Focus on them. Thank God for them and do it every day.

Gratitude will make you more attractive. There will be something about you that draws unspeakable opportunities your way.

When you start to develop an attitude of gratitude, it will improve your relationships with people. You won't be so consumed with envy that you'll be happy for others because you know what they have takes nothing away from you. People will sense that energy. You will attract good people who have the same attitude. Remember, you get to select your squad. Once you have your squad, those people you KNOW have your back and want you to succeed in life, appreciate them.

Take time to express gratitude to your parents for their sacrifices. If you're not good with words, write it down, or buy a card that expresses the sentiment of how you feel. Remember those who support you along the way in life. Teachers, counselors, coaches, mentors, friends, and supporters. Thank them often for how they invest in you and support you. You will feel so good when you do this. And you will help strengthen valuable relationships that will play a big part in helping you to become the person you are striving to be.

As we speak about gratitude, I want you to know that I am so thankful for YOU. I am thankful that you have allowed me the opportunity to speak into your life through this book. I don't take it lightly.

Thank you!

REFLECTION: What you are most grateful for right now? Why?

_____
_____
_____
_____
_____
_____

GO GETTER GOAL: Create a Gratitude List. Write down **EVERYTHING** and **EVERYONE** you are grateful for. Include experiences, lessons, memories, etc. Type it up. Create a picture or art piece with it. Place it somewhere you can see it daily. _____

_____
_____
_____

HIGH ACHIEVER CHALLENGE: Make a list of the people you are grateful for. Write them a note, buy them a thank you card, create an art piece, or simply send them a text/email/snap video expressing why you appreciate them. _____

_____
_____
_____
_____
_____

AFFIRMATION

"I am grateful!"

XII. Never Ever Quit

"Never, never, never give up." ~ **Winston Churchill**

<u>From My Journal:</u>

Don't Quit
A poem by John Greenleaf Whittier

When things go wrong as they sometimes will;

When the road you're trudging seems all uphill;

When funds are low and debts are high;

And you want to smile but you have to sigh.

When all is pressing you down a bit-

Rest if you must, but don't you quit.

Success is failure turned inside out;

The silver tint on the clouds of doubt;

And you can never tell how close you are;

It may be near when it seems far.

So stick to the fight when you're hardest hit-

It's when things go wrong that you must not quit.

Look Up and Beyond Strategy #12: Never Ever Quit

I'm so glad you made it to the end of this book. I hope this journey has been one of encouragement and inspiration and sparked in you the belief that you CAN overcome the tough times in your life. Storms don't last forever, and because of that, you can come out of the storms stronger and become the person you were meant to be.

This book should not be the end of your personal growth journey. Along with your academic knowledge and the skills you learn for your career path, make sure you stay open to personal development. Be intentional about reading good, positive, and empowering books. Take time to be self-aware. Do this often, and I promise you, your life will be better for it.

To recap, remember:

- You are unique. When you start to feel insecure, look at your fingerprints.

- You are valuable. When you question your worth, remember that no one can do what you do the way that you can do it. This makes you so valuable. See that same value in others.

- Spend your energy and time focusing on what you CAN control. Don't consume yourself with the actions of others. Be responsible for you. That includes choosing to have a positive attitude.

- Get and cultivate a vision for your life. Start thinking ahead about the person you want to be and the impact you want to make in the world. Envision it. Hold onto that vision.

- Select your squad carefully. Be cool and cordial with everyone but hang out with very few. Genuine friends are very rare. Never allow loneliness to push you into the lives of people you know are destructive. Find a mentor and be teachable.

- Avoid future regret. Strive to make good choices daily. You won't avoid mistakes entirely, but you can minimize making them if you think before you act. Take responsibility for yourself and own all of your actions.

- Manage your emotional pain during a crisis and times of distress. Forgive people who hurt you. Do it for you, not them. Monitor the things you watch, listen to, and read and stay conscious of how they affect your emotions. Get rid of things and people that cause negative emotions. Take time to self-care. You deserve it.

- Set goals. Work on 2-3 goals on any given quarter of the year. Be specific. Take action. Utilize the resources and support you have access to.

- Face your fears. Admit them. Study them to understand why you have them. Then let them go. The emotion of fear is not something you can get rid of entirely, but you don't have to be held prisoner by it anymore.

- Turn your pain into purpose. Identify your WHY. When you do, you'll figure out HOW.

- Be grateful for all the good things in your life. You are more blessed than you realize. Get rid of jealousy and the habit of comparing yourself to others. Gratitude will strengthen you for the journey.

- Decide today, that you will NEVER ever quit. When you're tired, rest but don't quit.

You are stronger than you think. And with these strategies, you will become *unstoppable.*

REFLECTION: What is that obstacle or thing that tries to make you quit? Identify it. _____

_____

_____

_____

_____

_____

GO GETTER GOAL: What is your biggest takeaway from this book? Explain. _____

_____

_____

_____

_____

_____

_____

_____

HIGH ACHIEVER CHALLENGE: What actions have you already taken to improve your life? What will you do next to ensure that you stay on this journey of growth (what book will you read/ who will you ask to be your mentor)?

_____

_____

_____

_____

AFFIRMATION:

"I am unstoppable!"

Acknowledgements

This book is very very special to me. I wrote it with so many incredible students and young people in mind- including my own children.

Thank you, Kayla, Kyle Jr. and Jared, - you inspire me so much. I want to be one of your greatest examples of resiliency, purpose and success. You are my greatest example of potential and possibility.

I have to say a big THANK YOU to my husband Kyle Janniere, who gets a front row seat to all of my behind the scenes "drama" during the book writing process. I love and respect you immensely and appreciate all the support you give me. I am effective in the work I do- in my purpose- because of your presence in my life.

Special thanks to Arel Moodie for writing the foreword. Your example, mentorship and friendship has changed my life. You are AWESOME!

I consider myself a student- a student of life, because I will never stop learning, growing and challenging myself to become more. To the teachers, mentors and coaches that have poured into me through the years- THANK YOU! I promise to pay it forward always.

Thank you to every person who endorsed my book- your support means the world to me.

I am so grateful for my squad; the friends and supporters I have in my life. You make the journey more bearable during those tough times and overall more fun and exciting. I can't do what I do alone. Nor do I want to!

I am very thankful to the students who offered feedback about the book. However, there is one young lady who went above and beyond; her name is Colleen James. Thank you, Colleen! You are a precious gem.

Lastly, if you purchased this book for yourself or someone else- THANK YOU! Your support is part of a powerful movement that is positively changing the lives of students all over the world.

Who Is Jessica Janniere?

Jessica Janniere is the author of "My Colored World" and the founder of Look Up and Beyond Inc. As a child abuse and rape survivor, Jessica is on a mission to help people to realize that negative past experiences do not equal a negative future regardless of the level of trauma they've faced.

Jessica is widely recognized as an expert in helping people (especially women and youth) overcome adversity. The New York State Assembly and Senate has recognized Jessica for raising awareness about, and improving the prevention of, suicide from individuals struggling with depression and emotional pain.

Her strategies have been so effective that she was awarded the prestigious "I Am Hope" Leadership Award, recognizing her ability to prevent human suffering. She has also been awarded the "Hope and Appreciation" Award by Opportunities and Change for helping women with mental health challenges. The New York City Council called Jessica a "Woman Who Makes a Difference."

Jessica has spoken to audiences ranging from 3 to 3,000 people, and she has shared the stage with celebrities like Ed Lover, one of MTV's most famous VJs. Jessica's work has been featured in numerous media outlets including the inspirational international magazine, Hope For Women. She has also been invited to appear as a guest expert on a variety of television shows to discuss overcoming past trauma.

Her dedication to helping people from all walks of life led her to her passion project of helping people during the darkest moments of their lives. Jessica has been on call 24/7 to help men and women who are in crisis and/or most at risk for committing suicide.

One of her greatest passions is working and speaking with youth who have challenging backgrounds to help them realize there is more to life than what they see in front of them. Through her "Look Up and Beyond: Youth Initiative," Jessica organizes outings to take inner city youth beyond the walls of their neighborhoods, many for the first time, to experience firsthand the amazing opportunities that exist in life.

Jessica is no stranger to success. She became one of the youngest Recreational Therapy Directors ever at a nursing home in New York City where she ensured that the elderly residents could live out the rest of their lives with passion, purpose and amazing quality of life. From there Jessica worked for one of the country's largest legal companies where she was one of the top recruiters and event planners for 10 years.

When Jessica isn't traveling the country to speak and her latest research, she can be found laughing with her family, riding the country's best roller coasters, completing adult coloring books and singing ... although she is still very shy about the last hobby :)

Conclusion

I would love to hear from you. Send me an email at jessicajanniere1@gmail.com and let me know how this book impacted you and/or if you are looking for a mentor.

You can read my full story by ordering *My Colored World: A Memoir* on Amazon.